Pour Me Another Cup

Pour Me Another Cup

Mystical Writings to Illuminate Your Soul

Stephanie Acello

Pour Me Another Cup:
Mystical Writings to Illuminate Your Soul
Heart Writing Series

Published by One Tone Publications, Colorado

ISBN: 978-1-7328533-0-0

Spiritual / Mystical Poetry / Meditations

Consultant: Polly Letofsky
Editor: Bobby Haas
Cover design: Dominic Acello and Andrea Costantine
Layout design: Andrea Costantine
Author photo: Sylvia Hooper

QUANTITY PURCHASES: Schools, companies, professional groups, clubs, and other organizations may qualify for special terms when ordering quantities of this title. For information, email stephanie.acello@gmail.com or visit www.StephanieAcello.com.

This book is printed in the United States of America.

One Tone
PUBLICATIONS

To my son, Dominic,
and the teachers, family, and friends
who offered support and contrast

ACKNOWLEDGMENTS

I would like to acknowledge a few people who were especially helpful in the creation of this book. First, love and gratitude to my son, Dominic, for taking the time from his busy schedule to design the book cover. Much appreciation goes to Andrea Costantine, the interior book designer, for her patience and guidance for a challenging layout design. I'm also grateful for Bobby Haas, my editor, who allowed me to explore my author's voice with patience and understanding. And the one woman who started the ball rolling, Polly Letofsky of *My Word Publishing,* for her support and guidance as a publishing consultant. Lastly, Sylvia Hooper, who generously offered to take my author photo.

Thanks to my local writing group for providing a forum to express my writings. I would also like to send my gratitude to Jennifer Grace, Hay House published author of *Directing Your Destiny,* for her writing and self-discovery workshops and bringing together a wonderful community of conscious woman.

Finally, thanks to all my human teachers and gurus who inspired and opened my Soul and to my animal and plant gurus who opened my Heart.

TABLE OF CONTENTS

Introduction

Step over the threshold
and allow the beauty of the mystical
to embrace you

Pour Me Another Cup: Mystical Writings to Illuminate Your *Soul* is a collection of *Heart Writings* reflecting the essence of life. These writings are an attempt to communicate the message of Heart and Soul into language. Each *Heart Writing* is an expression of a new consciousness that is surfacing along with a new vision of the world: a world vision shifting from the individual to the universal—from the personal self to the Absolute Self and most importantly, from the dream state of illusion to the awakened state of consciousness. A new world vision infused with the perception that celebrates individual uniqueness along with the awareness of Divine Oneness.

Humanity's consciousness is at a critical point in history, balancing on a very thin line of choice in deciding what kind of world we want to live in. Do we want to live in a world of fear and bondage or a world of love and freedom? Let it be known: within our power, we have the ability to lift the veil of illusion and embrace our role as co-creator with Eternal Source to develop a thriving and loving world. *Pour Me Another Cup* presents the opportunity to begin this shift of awareness by offering dynamic, inspirational, and profound insights on every page.

The *Heart Writings* do not follow conventional written rules; they are uncensored communication from the frequency of Heart and Soul, exposing the Inner Secrets and Data of the Mystical Realm that we all yearn to know.

These messages bypass both ego and thoughts; they process a higher vibrational awareness of Eternal Source and the Creative Intelligence underlying the whole order of existence: a vibration that is everyone's birthright.

As a special education teacher, I had to think outside the box to present the subject matter in a way that would be understood by the students. Many of the children did not have the confidence or background knowledge to comprehend the curriculum. Out of necessity, I became a master of taking the most complex subject matter and transforming it into material that was uncomplicated and understandable to my students. I believe this practice of simplifying information gave me the pathways to express the Inner Realms with uncomplicated simplicity that could be easily understood.

When in alignment with Eternal Source, information is not from the thinking realm, it is from the receiving realm: receiving awareness from the expansive perspective of life. To emphasize and honor this awareness, some words are capitalized and italicized within the writings. When a large section of the *Heart Writings* are italicized, it represents a Receiving Block of information or download of direct Awareness. Also, for a deeper comprehension of the writings, a glossary is added at the end of the book to clarify selected words and terms that are used in the *Heart Writings*. *Pour Me Another Cup* is a unique book to uplift and align with your higher consciousness. With this book, alignment does not require years of study or contemplation. This is a practical handbook that accommodates your time and desire; turn to any page or any section and allow the shift to take hold immediately.

The *Heart Writings* are to be read slowly and deliberately to yourself, quietly or out loud. After reading, take a moment to contemplate the writing you just read. You may even want to read it over again. The *Heart Writings* are from the vibration of Eternal Source and speak the universal language that touches the human spirit and sings the song of transcendence.

In addition to the *Heart Writings,* each chapter includes a *Sacred Moment Meditation* that offers an opportunity to engage in an experiential understanding of the chapter's focus and vision.

The *Sacred Moment Meditations* are contemplative activities and visualizations to stir and connect to your Inner Being in just a few moments.

Allow the *Heart Writings* to ignite and the *Sacred Moment Meditations* to fan the fire of remembering who you are and, most importantly, who you are Becoming.

The language of Heart speaks to you intimately
However
the message is universal

∽

HOW TO USE THE SACRED MOMENT MEDITATIONS

Each chapter focuses and communicates an insight from a higher vibration of consciousness. At the end of each chapter, a *Sacred Moment Meditation* is included. The meditations offer an experiential opportunity to engage in a deeper understanding of the chapter's subject—within minutes.

The following are *Sacred Moment Meditation* guidelines:

1. The *Sacred Moment Meditations* can be used after you read one or more *Heart Writings*. They can also be used independently.
2. Find a comfortable, quiet, and distraction-free area.
3. Sit on a chair, with your back relaxed and straight, with both feet on the floor. You can also lay on your back or sit crossed-legged in a yoga lotus position.
4. *Read The Sacred Moment* on the chapter's subject.
5. Next, read *The Sacred Moment Meditation* at least once.
6. Close your eyes and follow the meditation in your mind's eye.
7. If you have to open your eyes to check the sequence of the meditation, do so.
8. The meditations are about three to five minutes long and they are a great way to start the day. However, they can be done at any time, or any amount of times.
9. Most importantly, have fun!

I drank the passion of your Beingness

I'm drunk
I'm sick
I'm confused and baffled

Yet
pour me another cup

⸎

1

Boogie Your Way into Immortality

The beat of the heart represents the pulse of consciousness

All of creation is a rhythm

A pulse

A musical rhythm of different expressions
of the same Sound

You too
are an expression of the same Sound

A Sound singing the vibration of Eternal Source

Watch the rhythm
The pattern of hide and seek
Between
the realms of day and night
rising and falling of breath
and the beat of the heart

All are expressions of the eternal beat

Let it rock you
Let it lead you
And boogie your way into immortality

❧

The atom is the basic unit of matter
Vibrating tones

Each thing that is identified and labeled in the physical world
originated from thought

The thought is the basic unit of manifestation
Vibrating tones

The atoms are summoned by the power of thought
to join together and represent the idea of that thought
This is called a symbol

The symbol plays the tone to be sensed and perceived

Listen to the music

The tone of trees
The tone of clouds
The tone of river

Each person is also a tone
Do not listen to the words spoken
Listen to the music played

The questions to ask:

What is your tone?
What are your thoughts?

Is the music you are playing
in tune with the Symphony or not?

Water assumes the shape of its container

Spirit
like water
assumes the shape of its Being

What shape are you offering Spirit to fill?

Spirit does not have a home of its own

Spirit
like water
flows

Awaiting direction from you
Awaiting Home from you

☙

The ground we stand on is not solid
It moves with the sight we see

Its soil is made from beliefs
Hardened thoughts
This makes up our world
You can dig and dig
and the truth will never be found

Similar
to an artist who molds a vase out of clay
and an admirer searches in the clay
to understand how it was made
Impossible to do

You cannot see the spot you are standing on
Move out of the way

Float

Recognize the spot from the Above View

The power of belief is at your command
and sets the ground you stand on

A ground that is with you
no matter where you are standing

⌒ᖗ⌒

Ask a question
and the answer follows immediately
Questions and answers are on different banks
of one stream

The *Master* You knows this

All the questions asked have the same answer
They are within the inhalation and exhalation
of the same air

When you exhale the question
you need to inhale the answer
If you stay on the exhale
the inhale will never be

If you keep asking a question
there is no room for the answer
It is an extended exhale
and becomes extremely uncomfortable

Questions and answers are rhythmic
Ask
Receive
Ask
Receive

The question opens the channel to the Field of expansion
Receiving the answer allows the walk in this Field

Walking with a smile because the answer and question
are no longer important

◦͡◦

Closing one chapter
opens a new one
The finish of one thing
begins the start of another

Within each beginning
there is an ending
Within each ending
there is a beginning

It is inevitable that every life will experience death
But it is also inevitable
that every death will experience Life as well

The death of idea
The death of belief
The death of action
The death of body
All lead to a new Life

A Life that does not depend on living
Yet
it is the dormant basis of existence

A Life that is with you
while in this world or not

Spinning and circling the
Light of Love

THE CURRENT

The rhythm of life permeates the universe. It expresses itself in the beat of the heart, the movement of the sunrise and sunset, and the inhalation and exhalation of the breath.

These expressions of the Eternal Current run through all of existence. It is what allows existence to exist. The Current is constant and eternal even when the body perishes. It is at the beck and call for those who wish to connect. All that is needed to do is turn your attention to it. Once known, the Being surrenders and the Knowledge is reinstated.

Humans have free will to move their arms and legs. They also have free will to focus attention wherever and whenever they choose.

The only decision that ever has to be made is the decision to turn your attention to this Current. All falls into place and the choice to ride the waves of freedom are within every moment.

⌒⌒

Observe the eloquence of life's process

The grace of swan in flight
The power of horse in gallop
The gentleness of bee in each blossom
The wonder of leaf unfolding

All in tune to an internal
beautiful and rhythmic musical composition

The rhythm of the heart
The rhythm of the ocean's waves
The rhythm of day into night and night into day
The rhythm of the seasons
The rhythm of your walk and talk

The musical composition is the essence of your Being

You see
we are the music of the one Sound

A sound heard
but not from our ears
A sound seen
but not from our eyes
A sound silently loud

This is the sound of Sound
When it is felt
what has been forgotten is suddenly heard

What sound is this?
The Sound of Love

∽⚬∾

How do you live in a system that is designed
to keep you in ignorance?
A system that supports separateness
resulting in judging and bondage

Where is this system?
Is it in the schools and government
religion and family
culture and society?

This system sets the rules for your personal self to be accepted
into this elite club of conditioned beliefs
The ones you love passed it on to you
It is time to reveal Santa Claus
And to know magick does live
However
it is not in the system

Feel free to know that the system
is not what is holding the world together

Let go of the system within yourself
And do not listen to its voice
You can distinguish it by its tones of fear and ignorance

The system appears to be large and powerful
The power lies in the collective belief
that it is powerful

Once you realize the true power is not in the system
the system become submissive and turns to you for guidance

⤳⤳

SACRED CONVERSATION

Question: How do I trust myself?
Answer: *Acknowledging the rhythm of The Way*
Always a returning motion

Question: What is The Way?
Answer: *To know yourself*

Question: This seems difficult. How do I know myself?
Answer: *To know yourself*
you *must listen*
To listen
you *must be still*
In order to be still
you *must trust yourself*

See? It's easy

⤳

LOVE'S HUMMING

A young man was wandering through the mountains. He came from an affluent family, had a home, and was healthy. But he was sad and confused, always questioning his existence and purpose. He had an emptiness in his heart. He would ask everyone he met, "Who am I? What is my purpose?"

People would turn away from this man, feeling bewildered and even scared. One day, he saw a woman on the path who looked spiritual. She had long hair and was looking up to the sky.

He asked, "Please tell me: Who am I? What is my purpose?"

She turned and said, "How should I know? I am looking for some berries up in the tree to eat. Do you have any food?"

"I only have food for me," said the young man.

"Be gone with you." And she waved her hand at him in disgust.

He continued walking down the path and saw an old man with a long gray beard sitting on a rock. He looked peaceful and happy, while humming a strange tune. The young man even thought he saw a twinkle in the old man's eyes, but he quickly dismissed it and looked away. "Sir, I have a question for you."

The old man turned slowly and looked at him and said, "Yes."

"Who am I? What is my purpose?"

The old man paused and asked, "If I tell you, will you give me some money? I need a place to stay tonight."

"I do not have any money to give to you," said the young man and walked away, complaining under his breath.

The young man was always in a state of confusion in his mind and thoughts—always looking outside of himself for answers, never appreciating the beauty of the mountains, aspen trees, flowers, or the light in the eyes of all whom he met.

He continued to walk on the path and turned the corner and the same old man that he met earlier was sitting on a rock … humming. "How did he get ahead of me on the path?" he thought to himself.

The old man again asked for some money.

"Stop bothering me. I am not giving you anything." He walked away so quickly, he broke into a run. A little further down the path, he saw the old man again. Feeling scared, he turned around, hoping the old man would not see him. He started running in the opposite direction and was not looking where he was going; he tripped and fell to the ground. And lo and behold, when he picked up his head, there was the old man, sitting on a rock, smiling and humming.

"Do you have some money? I will answer your questions."

The exhausted young man said, "Well, all right." He proceeded to ask the questions but did not really believe he would get the answers he was seeking.

"Who am I and what is my purpose?" he asked in a bored tone.

The old man asked him to sit down on a rock beside him. "Now listen closely, not with your mind, with your heart." The old man started speaking, the tone was different, yet the voice was familiar. However, his lips were not moving as he spoke:

The Soul is the vessel for Spirit to flow
When the two merge
Identity arises
This is the Holy Marriage the sacred texts mention

The Soul is the matrix or blueprint for Identity

The Identity gives ground to personality
but it is not the personality
It is the dream of Becoming
in collaboration with the movement and rhythm of Spirit
The Soul is your connection to All That Is with
purpose being represented in your human form
The Soul is the authentic you and the expression of Self-love
Its depth is beyond the personal mind

The personal mind abides by the rules of logic and duality
The Soul does not have the same rules
it abides by the love of Self and gives direction from passion

Your Identity is not that you are rich or poor
pretty or ugly
successful or not
Your Identity is Eternal Source and
Soul allows the individual recognition of its Magnificence
through you
Your Identity far exceeds the limits of the body

Love is the reason for all desires
From the seed of tree to human birth
to grow and expand
Love is the heat of life which the Soul contains

The old man looked into the young man's eyes, and then spoke with his voice, "Love's Identity is You and Soul knows this. Who are you? And what is your purpose?"
"Your Identity is a lover."
"Your purpose is to love."

The young man felt like he got shot with a bolt of lightning and all of sudden noticed the beauty around him: colors bursting, fragrances in the air, and the soft caress of the wind on his face. He also heard all around him the tune the old man was always humming. He felt love for the old man and, most importantly, he felt love for himself. He put his arm around the old man and said, "Come, I have a place for you to stay."

Within every moment
Presence of Consciousness is standing by
allowing the surfacing of Awareness

Thus
the moment becomes sacred

All looks slightly brighter
Movement is in slower motion
Time has no effect

The perimeter of the surroundings is gently yelling
I AM I AM I AM

The heart starts to pump wildly with excitement
Heat rising

You are filled with your Divine Identity

And there is nothing else left to do
other than
bow your head and open your heart

⤞⤝

Looking for the secret of life
is the insatiable quest for meaning and purpose

It has been written in the ancient texts of the East and West
It has been passed down from indigenous people from
the world's four quarters with the following message:

You *co-create the life that lives through* you
It is from the power of your *thoughts and beliefs*
The Love from Eternal Source *allows the direction* you *set*
This is your *birthright*
Love is the essence of all existence

The Voices of the past have said it all:

I AM
Great Spirit whose breath gives life to all the worlds
Ask and it is Given
Thy Will Be Done
The Tao is the Source of ten thousand things
Ehyeh Asher Ehyeh
So Ham

The outer world is the projection of the inner worlds
And the essence of all things is *Eternal Source*
No matter what label or name is placed on them

This has been known for eons

So the secret of life
is not such a secret after all

❦

Dance in the moonlight
Sing with the bird songs
Sway with the wind and clouds
Feel the pulse of Mother Earth

She holds and cradles you
And rocks you softly in her arms
Nothing is still
other than *That* which underlies movement

To live
the movement must be felt
To be alive
the stillness must be felt

All movement springs from one Stillness
All movement springs from one Stillness

The eternal movement and pulse
can only be experienced within Stillness
It is cyclical
Pulse is from Stillness
Stillness moves to Pulse
and Pulse leads back to Stillness
Revealing no separation
Therefore all is holy
This is the paradox of life

Rock with Mother
Feel the Pulse of Heart while in her arms
and allow the movement to take you Home

SACRED MOMENT ON
IMMORTALITY

Take a moment and watch your breath: the inhalation and exhalation. It is the ultimate rhythm of life. *That* which moves your breath, moves the Earth around the sun. It is *That* which the trees reach for and *That* which fills your Heart.

Your breath is a direct line to Eternal Source—*That* which moves your breath connects the inner and outer worlds. The secret of the rhythm of life will be known through the breath.

MEDITATION

Sit and take a moment and bring your awareness to your breath. Listen to your breath. Gently close your eyes and breathe in slowly on the count of four. Hold the inhale for a moment, then exhale slowly on the count of five, and hold the exhale for a moment. Do this five times comfortably; then breathe normally.

While breathing normally, focus on the rhythm of the rising and falling of the breath for a couple of minutes: this is the expression of the sacred rhythm of consciousness. Repeat if you wish. Slowly open your eyes and continue the day or evening, knowing you are a projection of Eternal Source, dancing to rhythm of life.

2

~❦~

LOVE LOVE AND
LOVE WILL LOVE YOU

The world is filled will nothing
Nothing is filled by you
Now take a deep breath and hear Love's Voice

Making love
heightens your awareness

Making love
lasers through the dimensions to a higher vibration
Where time and space no longer exist

Making love
is the vehicle to ride to the heavens
and to know what you always wanted to know
and to feel what you always wanted to feel

Make love to all that you encounter
whether it be your
lover and family
pen and dance
canvas and song

Through the making of love
quietly and joyfully

Love is making you

⤸

Unconditional Love
is not love that fits your standards
Your standards make it conditional

Some feel with all the diversity
in beliefs and practices that are now
coming out
is a warning of society's destruction

True
there is confusion

However
it is time to love unconditionally

To stand firm within yourself
and not stand in the way of others

Stand on the mountaintop and watch
the cycle of the Sacred Gear
emptying to be filled

Confirming
the *coming out* is the beginning of
going in

❧

BUTTERFLIES IN SPACE

There once was a mother who loved her son very much. She raised him on her own and always kept him safe. She loved to cook for him, and they spent many days in nature when he was young. The beach, woods, and mountains were the playing grounds for them.

The son had a quick intellect, an affinity for music, and a kind heart. But his father left suddenly, and his young mind did not understand. His mother wanted to protect him from the hurt and pain.

She surrounded him with friends, vacations, and activities, hoping to fill the void that was starting to develop within him. As he got older, he became more distant, and the scene between them was always the same:

"I have dinner ready for you; it is your favorite," said the mother with a big smile on her face.

"I am not hungry. I have to go out," replied the son in an agitated voice. "Do you have money? I need cigarettes."

The mother reached into her purse and gave him what she had.

He turned away quickly and walked out of the house. He never said "thank you". He never even bought her a card on her birthday or asked if she needed any help with her chores.

One day out in the fields, the mother was carrying a heavy load, and he passed her without a glance and did not even offer a hand of help. She felt very sad.

"This is not love; this is fear repeating the same old patterns of protection," she said to herself. "My son's actions are telling me my protection is not love, and it is causing him pain." She paused and asked herself, " What is love?" And she looked up to the heavens.

One day, she sat in contemplation by the river. She watched the butterflies flying from one flower blossom to another. No butterflies were interfering with other butterflies concerning where and when to fly ... all moving freely.

The mother noticed that some butterflies would go to a flower blossom that was dying or a flower of a weed. The butterflies knew which blossom to take the nectar to pollinate other flowers for the seeds of continuation. They saw the beauty in the blossom, even if she did not.

"The butterflies know how to maintain the balance for the love of nature," she whispered to herself.

The insight came to her:

Love cannot be contained
Love cannot be controlled
To love is to be a witness to the beauty and allow it to be
Love and letting go are true partners

In that moment, she felt free and full of love. She let go of all the sadness, protection, and judgments. She reached in her pocket and released all her butterflies into space.

⸦ⸯ

It is known when the Universe moves through you

You know this when love is felt
and the breath is *Breathed* without you

The Universe is moved by and through Love

When separate
you are an island of limited resources
You turn
The door is closed

Love is the space for unlimited potentiality
You turn
The door is open

Circling without a beginning or ending

❧

Light your candle with love
inspiration and passion

You will light the world

The winds of thought must die down
for the flame to burn brightly

Clear your mind of breezy thoughts

One candle lights the whole room
One being lights the whole world

Oxygen is the fuel for the flame
Love is the fuel for life

Nothing else is needed

Life could never happen without love
There would be no reason to live

All motives and intentions are from love
From the seed of a tree to the Earth's circling of the sun

In other words
All That Is in the physical and nonphysical realms
are Love's projections
When anything is acknowledged
know that love is behind it
That You are behind it

The illusion of life's motion is from the Eternal Source's desire
to experience more of itself through you

When you stay in the state of love
you are in the state of grace

This is when you feel the presence of angels
and become familiar with your subtle dimensions

Linear becomes depth
Depth becomes more in the Now

Within the Now
is the only journey of life

⤞⤝

A soul mate is a mate of Soul

Heart sings a familiar song
when recognizing your*Self* in the other

An unspoken encounter known before time

The sun and shadows mix upon the Earth
The divine dance of light and dark
Dancing to the music of Love

Soul mates
are two physical forms
who are *in Love*
but not with each other

When abducted by love
you no longer have a mind that takes the lead

The heart yearns to be One
and the mind has no say

Openness eats all in and takes hold of touch
No words will be spoken
Just breath to breath
Mouth to mouth
Taking each in
Allowing each out

This is the intoxication of the universal process

To open
give
receive
and merge back into Ecstasy

In the presence of Love
nothing is required or expected

In the flux of time
past
present and future
dissolve

The Communication is open to receive
without the interference of the personal mind

The Heart swells
in anticipated acknowledgement of its power

Be present in the Present
This is Love's home

You search and search for what?
You want and want for what?
You look and look for what?
You cry and cry for what?
What is it that you crave and feel incomplete without?
It is love
You seek love
You yearn for love
You want love
You are afraid to love
You fear receiving love
You don't feel loved

Everything stems and rests in Love
All of existence exists out of Love
You think it is something you can get
No never
It is not to get
One cannot get something one already is
Actually
you don't even have it
It has you
Yet
It is itless
and cannot be contained
This is the nature of your*Self*
Look at your world
it holds the clues
When you see beauty
you are moved
Then ask the question:
What is it that moves you?

When you see a kind soul helping another
you are moved
What is it that moves you?
When you see a wondrous creation
you are moved
What is it that moves you?

This is the question to ask and the answer to receive

*It is the motion of Love rising to the occasion to be
experienced and remembered*

So when your lover comes home
kiss her and tell her you love her
Loving her
you will feel love

When your child comes home dirty
clean him with tenderness and tell him you love him
Loving him
you will feel love

Do something nice for yourself
Just for you
Loving you
you will feel love

Within these simple acts is what you are searching for
Love is staring you in the face
You are the lover
loving and loved

Love's expansion of the world allows the coasts to meet

The oceans and mountains will not be barriers
Love is deeper than the deepest ocean
and higher than the highest peak

The world's expansion is inevitable
Our expansion is inevitable

Love's motion is to encompass all
expanding from its *Original Focal Point*

This is where Love springs into existence
and allows the experience of its own Essence

∽

SACRED CONVERSATION

Question: What is unconditional love?

Answer: *When you are standing in the midst of a storm*
and love the way the wind feels on your face

❦

WALK THE PATH OF THE DIVINE

Love is not outside of you. You look for it in the other, and the other looks for it in you. The other cannot give you what you already are. However, if you do not feel the love within, love will not be felt, no matter how much love is shed upon you.

The experience of love of *Self* reveals the Eternal Love, which is the basis of existence. The Heart knows this. The tree reaches for the sun out of love. The bird sings its song out of love. A human breathes out of love. All of creation desires the experience of love.

When you are in a loving state, you are the closest to your GodSelf. Your life is an expression of the opportunity to experience love: a love that can only be felt from the perspective of the Ultimate Love. The Ultimate Love has no conditions, judgments, or attachments. Love can only see love. So move out of the way.

Loving *this or that* excludes *All That Is*, for you are loving just *this or that*. However, loving *this and that* includes *All That Is*. The sum total of all the love does not constitute the magnificence of Love's Source. You are an aspect or projection of what everything else is. Everything is love or it would not be.

Eternal Source shines the love with no judgment —the same way the sun shines on gold as well as on garbage with no judgment. It just shines and gives. Your life is the physical experience of love. Walk the path of the divine and fall deeply in love with your life.

When *We* speak of love
It is not the love of something or someone
It is the love that something or someone expresses

If all the love was accumulated
The love between humans
The love of nature to blossom
The love of birth
The love of giving
The love of service
it would not touch the love that is You

Love is what drives the cells to support the body
and the atoms to form the world

Love is even in fear
Its nemesis

The love of a child for its mother
may be the closest example of touching
the Love of Eternal Source
However
it is within all

So when *We* speak of love
We are speaking directly to You

The beautiful extension of Love's Arm

SACRED MOMENT ON
LOVE

Love is the basis of all existence. Its pulse is the beat of the heart. It is the reason the atoms are attracted to each other and form matter. It is the reason you have desires to expand and express more love of *Self*. It is the reason you choose to come into this physicality, and it is the same reason you will choose to leave.

MEDITATION

Gently close your eyes; inhale and exhale slowly for five cycles. Pay attention to the rising and falling of the breath. Focus on your heart center, and place your hands over your heart, one hand over the other. Breathe into your heart and feel gratitude for life, just to be living.

Continue to focus on your breath. Imagine your heart as a pink lotus flower, opening more and more with each inhalation. When it fully opens, know you are in a state of receiving *All That Is*. Stay with this feeling for a few moments. Slowly open your eyes and continue your day or evening with an open heart.

಴

3

Even the Seemingly Unimportant is Important

Everything you encounter from a grain of sand
to the Rocky Mountains speaks Truth
Everything has meaning even the meaningless

Significance is in all that you encounter
From the first breath at birth
to the last breath at death

See the word *sign* in *sign*ificance
There is something significant about the word significance

All you face in life is a *sign*
indicating and implying
expressing and conveying a meaning

Anything that is on your path
and calls for your attention is significant

Whether it be a small pebble or an infant child
Whether it be a blade of grass or your lover
Whether it be the feel of a breeze or the sight of an angel

Significance is *That* which has meaning and purpose
Meaning and purpose are within your Origin

Your significance is knowing how significant you are

Once known
even the dust on your shoes will be viewed with reverence

࿇

Maya
The word the yogis use to label
the illusion of life

Maya
The veil that separates the real from the unreal

Maya
The dreamlike state of the impermanence of life
mistakenly taken as permanent

Look deep within yourself

Like a still pond on a summer's day
the reflection of the trees
sky and clouds seem so clear and real
one could get lost

Look deep
beyond the reflection

Awaken from the hypnosis
Awaken from the dream

And See the Essence of what forms reality

❧

Past lives say exactly what they are
Past
Gone
Puff
Even if you chose to focus on the past
It is still happening
now
The only life to be lived

We are an accumulation of all of the energy of all the lives
However
we are only living and focusing on the one life that is now

When attention is put on any life energy
that energy will be experienced

The significance of the past is … *it was*
The significance of the present is … *it is*
The significance of the future is … *it will be*
The significance of all three is that they
exist only in the Now

When thoughts and feelings are in the past
You are reliving and staying in the past
Stuck
It is your choice

Your present life should be enough to keep you busy
If you want to invite energy into the present
invite what can become
not
what has already been done

SHINY THINGS

Down a dirt path alongside a lake on a bright autumn day, the discovery was about to be revealed.

The children screamed, "Look! Look at the *shiny things!*" as they pointed to the lake with full excitement.

I looked and said to myself, "What *'shiny things'* are they talking about?"

"What are they? Look how they stay on top of the water!" screamed the children, eyes wide open.

I then realized they were talking about the sun's reflection upon the rippled lake water. I was about to explain the scientific reason for this occurrence and correct them from *shiny things* to the sun's reflection.

The moment stood still.

I looked at their faces full of wonder and excitement. An excitement that I also shared while in search of these *shiny things*.

A Knowing washed throughout my body.

They are seeing the wonder and magic of life. I am seeing a concept.

An insight surfaced:

When I think I know something
it stops me from seeing what really is

We all sat by the lake's shore and watched in silence as the *shiny things* danced upon the water.

When importance is placed on the conditioned world
and demands your full attention
connection to Eternal Source is lost

It results in tunnel vision and leads to
confusion and discomfort

Desperately grasping a key to a keyless door

Suddenly
a light under the door invites a push

Upon entering
illumination penetrates and the tunnel dissolves

Once again
the breath is felt
well-being returns
and clouds roll by

Connection to Eternal Source is resumed
revealing what is truly important

❦

Doubt stands between living and thinking about living

Each circumstance rectifies
doubt or faith

If doubt wins
it gains strength from the focus on fear and distrust
You know this when your body stiffens and stands guard

When surrendering to faith
the opposite occurs
The focus is on love and trust
Body relaxes
Heart opens

And it is known that there is no more need for protection

᎐᚛᎐

Where do I begin?
At the beginning
How do I begin?
By doing
What do I do?
Stand out of the way

In the starting of anything
the illusion of the beginning appears
In the doing of anything
the illusion of the doer appears
However
the eternal process is beginningless and actionless
How can there be a beginning or end to the eternal?
How can there be a doing or not doing to *All That Is*

The beginning is *already*
The implication of the past
present and future does not exist
All exist only in the Now
The action is the physical effect
The doing has nothing to do with you

The ancient text knew the process
The Tao abides in non-action
Yet nothing is left undone

Imagine a stream containing all the glitter of possibilities
a dipping into *That* which is already propels the body
Similar to a puppet with a choice

THE SCARF

A troubled girl watched a sage, a holy person, before prayer. The sage proceeded to wrap a scarf around her shoulders as she lit the altar's candle. The girl asked, "Why do you put on that scarf?"

"It is like life itself. It is sacred," replied the sage.

The girl laughed. "Like life itself? Hardly! It is an old, ripped, ugly scarf, far from being sacred," the girl said with a disgusted face.

"Oh, my dear child," spoke the sage. "When I put on this scarf, it is a remembrance."

"A remembrance of what?" the girl blurted out. "That you need to do the laundry?" She laughed sarcastically.

The sage smiled, holding back a laugh, and continued to speak, "It is a remembrance of my true nature and where love originates. It is a remembrance of the beauty of a child's innocence and the soft whisper of a breeze. It is love."

A silence enveloped the room. The sage had a different look on her face and spoke with a soft tone:

Within love is sacredness
Within sacredness is consciousness
Within consciousness is presence and within Presence
I AM

The sage gazed at the young girl, who had a tear in her eye, and said, "You see, my child, like life itself, this is not just a scarf."

Every moment offers the opportunity
to throw a direct line to the *ships of thought*
and guide them to the *shore of circumstance*

Your attention and how important it is to you
opens the port and brings them in

*Import*ance is what you decide to
import into your life

There are no exports
Just imports

To make an export
you must import what you want
Not export what you do not want

It is a pier of only receiving

The ports are open
The *ships of thought* are waiting to deliver

This is the place of the Ultimate Decision

The captain approaching the pier yells out
Is this what you want?

SACRED CONVERSATION

Question: What is so important
that it pulls me away from You?

Answer: *Thinking there is a 'me'
that could be pulled away from a 'You'*

Waves of emotion
Motion sickness prevails

The highs allow the meaning
The lows the meaningless

Up and down
Down and up
Nausea persists

By riding on the surface
still waters are difficult to find
The searching causes disturbance

Dive deep and feel the sight of darkness

Then bob up and float on the waves of motion
Lie back with trust and love

And rest on what is truly holding you up

❦

Nothing ever has to be healed
To heal
implies that something is wrong and needs to be fixed
The focus is on what is wrong
Remember
focus cannot focus on what is not present
It only shines its laser in the direction of your attention
If it is wanted or not wanted

Healing is a process that has not yet become
Therefore
the focus is on *what is not*
Focus can focus on well-being
Our true nature is always in this state
It knows of nothing else
Well-being is always present
Therefore
the focus is on *what is*
Well-being is a forward motion with the support of
all of existence
Healing is a backward motion with the support of resistance

When well-being appears to be disrupted in our physicality
the natural movement has been blocked
Blocked by feelings
thoughts and actions against Spirit's Current
Against love
Embrace the block with love no matter how painful
It will dissolve and flow once again with Spirit
When this occurs
be prepared for the ride of your life

It is paramount
It is ultimate
It is imperative to know that the questions you hold have only
one answer
One answer only
A *question* is the *quest* for the answer
No matter what the question is
the answer is always the same

How can this be?
How can one answer be the answer for
all of the diversity of questions asked?
Why is there war?
Because there is *no* peace
Why is there violence?
Because there is *no* tolerance
Why is there so much hate?
Because there is *no* acceptance
Why is there confusion?
Because there is *no* understanding
Why is there so much fear?
Because there is *no* love

All the *no's* that stand in the way of peace and tolerance
acceptance and understanding
and love
negate and separate from God
All the *yes's* that embrace peace and tolerance
acceptance and understanding
and love
confirm and merge with God

The space between the *no's* is the separation
where the desire springs
and sets on a quest for the answer

The answer of *Yes* to Return
Return to Eternal Source
Return to Love
The answer is always *Yes*

⸎

Conscious awareness is a
moment when a whole being becomes Whole

Each object
living or not
becomes an old friend
that has been forgotten

Within the celebration of the union
a sadness prevails from forgetting such a good friend for so long

A good friend who has been waiting patiently for your attention

⌒⊶⌒

SACRED MOMENT ON
SIGNIFICANCE

Whatever draws your attention is significant. Pay attention to the thoughts and feelings that surface when something captures your attention. It is telling you about You.

Out of all the things you encounter in a day, wonder about the ones that call for your attention, from the most subtle to the most blatant. As you are walking, you may notice a butterfly, rock, or a bird singing. Your eyes may connect for a brief moment to a stranger on the street. Don't analyze, just observe and acknowledge the encounter. It is a calling of another kind saying, *Look here! I AM I AM I AM.* All is significant; no exceptions.

MEDITATION

Gently close your eyes; inhale and exhale slowly for five cycles; with each inhalation say to yourself, *I AM significant.* Next, breathe normally and visualize a scene in the forest for approximately two minutes. In your mind's eye, see the tall, majestic trees, ferns, flowers, creatures, and the rich, dark soil. Look around in your mind's eye, and observe how all is interconnected and interrelated: the trees and plants reaching for the sun's light and the bees and butterflies flying from flower to flower, ensuring the flower's existence. See the birds dropping seeds onto the soil for future trees and plants. Everything in nature depends on each other to continue the wonder of life.

Feel the warmth of the sun and the soft breeze on your face. Walk to a pond and look at the reflection of your face in the still waters. You are smiling because it is known that you are a significant aspect in this life as well.

Take a deep inhalation and exhale completely, breathe normally. Open your eyes slowly. Rest with Mother Earth, holding you in her palm, and continue the day or night knowing you are an integral part of life.

4

KNOCK KNOCK
WHO'S THERE?
YOU

Don't be afraid
Look deep
Open your eyes and Heart
and allow Self to know itSelf

The fear of fear is enormous
It is a runaway train coming directly toward you
as you stand immobile
All that you are running from is running with you
Not far behind

Fear is always by your side
You pretend it is not there and cover it up with
activity and distraction
Fear knocking at your door
An entity with its own agenda
What is that agenda?
What is fear's job?
What does it want?
These are the questions to ask

Fear keeps you from your Greater Self
if you resign to it
However
fear can lead you to your Greater Self
if you face it

This is the intention
Not to keep you *from*
but to lead you *to*

Look squarely in fear's eye
It is not your enemy
It is your guide

Your worst fear masks the most spectacular you
Fear is leading you to what you must face
The face of your Light
The face of your Love
The face of *All That Is*

Fear is knocking
not to come in
but to let you out!

What do you really have?

A home
Family
Money
Health
Happiness

All can disappear in a flash

Do you truly have anything?

Then what are you holding onto so tightly?

∽⚬∾

STAND ALONE

Be alone
You will never be lonely

Aloneness is to stand alone. This does not mean being isolated, quite the opposite. It means to stand on your own and assume responsibility for who you are.

All too often you judge and conduct your actions according to other's approval. These actions are not yours at all. You then live in a world separate from your desires and beliefs. *How lonely.* To stand alone means to stand on your beliefs, no one else's.

When you stand alone with yourself, you are one with yourself. Within the one is *All That Is*. When you are truly one with yourself, you are One with all of existence. So tell me, how can you possibly be lonely in this divine state?

Know
that who you are
is what everything else is

See and feel yourself in all of your surroundings
From the dandelion to your lover
You share something in common

The gift of life

When you look with sincerity
the looking becomes Seeing
then Seeing sees ItSelf

Fear subsides
because you can no longer be afraid of yourself

⚮

Looking in the mirror
I am staring at an unfamiliar face

Who is she?
She is not a reflection of how I see myself
She is not the one who is with me all day

What the hell happened?

I cannot put all my apples in this basket any longer

She is a stranger

This reflection is bouncing off light
But where is the light of the image coming from?

I need to see past the reflection

One thing I am sure of
the face I am seeing is not who I am

There must be a clue
Where am I?

The light in the eyes partly admits my existence
and confirms my Presence

Looking into my eyes
and the eyes are looking back at me

I start laughing
Here *I AM*

TWO EMOTIONS

Fear and love are the only two emotions that exist. Anger, sadness, anxiety, and rage all stem from fear, originating from feelings of not being loved or supported. Happiness, bliss, joy, and contentment all stem from love, originating from feelings of being loved and supported.

When an emotion is experienced, distinguish it from fear or love. If it is anything other than the feelings of *all is well,* know it is fear. This makes it very simple to distinguish.

Fear is experienced when you are separate from Eternal Source, separated by the wall of negative thoughts and non-serving, embodied beliefs. You are now floating in an uncertain, unsafe ocean ... sinking fast.

What keeps you afloat is your *lifeline* to Eternal Source. When you are in fear, know you drifted from your Connection ... you *are lost,* much the same as a child who wanders away from his mother in a store and then realizes he is alone. The store allured him by the illusion, capturing his attention to material things, and he disconnected from his mother. The child panics and experiences fear ... *he is lost.*

When the illusion of life is taken to be real, fear and chaos become part of the worldly reality. You lose your power. Your ally, fear, is the indicator that you drifted. It tells you, out of love, that you need to reconnect. It is your friend. Embrace it—and it will point in the direction to be found.

Fear's message is always the same.
Reconnect!

Once you have a relationship with fear, fear is not so fearful. Fear is an aspect of you. How can you be afraid of yourself? Listen and fine-tune your awareness so you can hear its first message. Actually, once you distinguish the two emotions and understand the language of fear, you will then know there is really only one emotion.

The emotion of love.

Impulse is the divine guidance
It is often overlooked

An impulse starts with a gentle *nudging and a soft whisper*
Feelings of inspiration and the emotion of love rises
Exposing the direction that is best for you

If not acknowledged
the impulse becomes a *poke and a quiet voice*
Feelings of sadness and fear may pop up
Situations will appear in your circumstance
to get your attention

If still not acknowledged
the impulse becomes a *shove and a loud voice*
Feelings of disconnect and emptiness may pop up
Bodily discomfort starts to appear

If it continues not to be acknowledged
the impulse becomes a strong *push and screams loudly*
Feelings of questioning your existence may pop up
resulting in unpleasant manifestations

Now
it has your attention
and gently nudges and whispers in your ear:

All I wanted you *to know is that*
I Love You

Fear develops when you invest
all time and energy
thoughts and actions
in the temporary
The fear of losing is always hanging around your neck

How can you hold on to impermanence?

Yet
the hold continues
the fear continues

Why not invest in the eternal?
The beginningless beginning
to the endless ending

Know your birthright

The worldly reality is for the mortal
The eternal reality is for the immortal

Which are you?

SACRED CONVERSATION

Question: How do I let go of the past and stop worrying
about the future?

Answer: *Accepting the Present*
is leaving the past behind
Accepting the Present
is dropping the worry of moving
toward the future

Accepting the Present
will bring a realization that there was
nothing to leave behind or move toward

◦⟋⟍◦

THE BOX

Deserving is the state of being worthy
To accept and love your image
as well as the Source of the image
It is to know the value of the Life that is living through you
It is the ultimate gift from the omnipresent Benefactor
A gift designed to be enjoyed by you and to share with others

An old man was standing on the street corner, begging for food and money from passersby. He felt the world was against him. A young, homeless boy approached the old man and pleaded to share some food or money with him.

The old man barked, "Can't you see that I do not have enough for me?"

The young boy hung his head in shame and walked away.

One day, a woman gave the old man a box, and he grumbled to himself, "A box; big deal."

She spoke to him kindly and said, "Serve in the name of Love and allow it to guide you. You will get all that you deserve. When you serve is when you are a Master."

He brushed her off and said, "Leave, woman!"

The box became his only home. And he sat on it day into night and night into day, through the rain and snow, complaining and grunting at every opportunity. Eventually, he became very sick and died a miserable old man.

The woman heard about his death and returned to the street corner. She realized he had never opened the box. The box was filled with money, jewels, and the deed to a home. "He was sitting on a treasure, and he didn't even know it. "What a shame!" she said to herself. She picked up the box and walked on.

∽

Know the distinction between
Purpose and purpose
Purpose is universal and purpose is individual
The desire for life's meaning
and to make a difference in the world
is what fuels them both
Purpose is not found outside of one's self
Individual purpose is very close to Heart
whispering the Story of universal *Purpose*
The ultimate reason for existence
Every participant of life has a unique path or individual purpose
And only by following your path
will it reveal the universal *Purpose*

The daisy's Becoming is what creates
the precise balance and beauty
against the backdrop of the Whole Picture of nature
If the daisy did not bloom
it would not be in the Picture

Purpose is all the same from the flower to the human
sharing the journey of Becoming
And only within the flourishing of its individual purpose
is the Story known

To look for it
purpose is lost
To Be it
Purpose is found

CՏ

Authenticity is not to be reached
It is to settle within and be worthy of acceptance

Authenticity uses the unreal of the world's reality
to adjust to the *real* of your Originality

Therefore
it is a continuous stretching of rising and falling

Authenticity is rooted in honesty and awareness
This is where the Voice is heard
And indicates to the personal self
the distance from the *Eternal Self*

When one is authentic
the Soul is a close partner

The Soul gives direction in the language of inspiration
And inspiration gives the path for expression

A path that only the Authentic Self can walk on

⌇

I feel safety within the confines of my prison
My prison offers me the boundaries of myself
and the scope of my travel

Spending my life cursing this prison
Yet
when the opportunity arises
I dare not leave

This prison was constructed to protect me
What a good job it's done
But
what has it protected me from?

I thought it was the pain
hurt and sadness
Actually
it protected me from love
joy and expansiveness

Why do I need protecting?

Who is the enemy?

I look in the mirror and all I see is me

Don't fear
fear

Fear is the messenger
Singing the message of *what* you *are not*
It wants to be released

When an animal is caged
all food and shelter is given
The animal loses its instinct and forgets who it is

Like the animal
You too
are caged

Caged within your fears
Also
forgetting who you are

The cage is your story
Opening the gate is your birthright

SACRED MOMENT ON
FEAR

Fear is your ally. Embrace it and do not push it away. It is rising to the occasion to show you something about you. It wants to be released. That is why it is relentless about being recognized. Know on the flip side of fear is love. The love pushing through the resistance.

Your true nature is love and *All That Is*. Any fear that is experienced is the rejection of your Greater Self. Fear is the signpost that is pointing in the direction that you are seeking. Learn its language: *It is love that is missing* your *attention*.

MEDITATION

Bring awareness to your breath, and inhale and exhale slowly for five cycles. Next, take a few moments and think of one reason to have gratitude and appreciation. It could be your home, family, and friends. It could even be gratitude for the body that navigates you in this physical existence or just the fact that you are living.

Gently close your eyes and place your hands on your thighs, palms open and upward, and focus your attention on the open palms of your hands. Open hands are always ready to receive. Feel the energy in the palms of your hands. They may feel tingly, heavy, or nothing at all. Stay with your focus on your palms for a minute or two in silence.

Slowly open your eyes and look at your open hands and know that fear cannot live when you are in a state of appreciation, gratitude, and receptivity. Bring your hands together in a prayer position, and bow your head to allow the Magnificence of life to rise.

❦

5

SERVE YOURSELF THE WHOLE COURSE

The only way to give of yourself is to Be yourself

Service is the next step

Once you serve yourself
by listening to your dreams and desires then acting upon them
the rising tide extends outward for others to share
To share the love you found in yourself

This is true service

The love of *Self* has to come first
before you can truly love another

If your service is from a place of lack
then the serviced will always feel in need

If your service is from a place of more
then the serviced will feel empowered

True service is not helping other beings
whether a person
animal or plant
as though they are helpless

True service is the extension of love
which offers the opportunity for the other
to connect with Eternal Source
through you

⤜⤏

Perfection is not performing actions perfectly
Impossible to exist

Perfection cannot be judged from a reference point
It is a knowing
not a result

It is linked with authenticity
Authenticity is linked with love

Therefore
the state of perfection is love

Authenticity is a clear pool
witnessing the depths of your *Beingness*
Thus
becoming a reflection to enable others to witness
the depths of their *Beingness*
Saturated with the wetness of Insight

This is the most you can give someone
Your Authentic Self

⸎

All is well
even when it appears to be not well
Attune to the music of the plants and trees

The only place to be
is in Being
Turn your attention within the Now
The senses can help
Feel the breeze
Smell the aroma
Hear your breath

Within Being
is the *coming to Be*
It includes All and it is the only constant

Being is a dynamic static experience
When in the state of Being
no boundaries exist between the dimensions
of the here and the beyond

You do not experience a circumstance
as though there is a you and a *circumstance*

*Circum*stance is a part of the
Sacred Circumference
This is the Cycle's workings

Simultaneously
the *energy form* of your thoughts and beliefs are extended
and expressed as *physical form* in the manifested world

Once the form is perceived by the mind
a returning motion occurs to experience the circumstance
A circumstance you set in motion
Therefore
in every circumstance is the experience of yourself

Yourself is within Being
Where All exists including your Becoming

Observe nature
The tree is anchored in the Now
Yet
it is becoming more of what it is each moment
When the fruit is grown
this is the tree's circumstance
and it is not separate from the tree

The state of Becoming is within Being
By being in the Now
you are inviting the coming to Be as You
With no outside interference
This mysterious funnel of creation is when you are in the
eye of the storm
and the winds circle but dare not enter

&

What is
isn't
what it is

Life is constant movement
Dynamic
With the illusion of stationary
Static

The Earth is in
rotation and revolution
Yet
we feel it not

The reoccurrence of the same creation enhances the illusion
of sameness and permanence

The choice of creation starts the
momentum of the becoming of *what is*

What is
is the product of *what was*
that you are choosing to continue to become

‿ᑯ‿

SACRED CONVERSATION

Question: How can I be a servant to God?

Answer: *By becoming a Master of yourself*

⤟

SELFISH IS THE WAY

A young student under the tutorage of a sage asked the question, "Why is it so important to perform selfless service?"

"Because it is *Selfish*!" replied the sage.

"Selfish?" said the student. "How could selfless service be selfish? When I perform a service, I ask for nothing in return, even though it is my time, money, and action. I am not doing it for myself. I am doing it to help the other. How could my service be selfish?"

The sage smiled and stated, "When you truly perform a selfless act, there is no separation from the other. That is why it feels good to service another. The *Self* of the other is the *Self* of you. As you serve another, you are servicing yourself." The sage directed his eyes back to the student and waited patiently for a reply.

"But isn't it bad to be selfish?" replied the student.

"It matters which self you are referring to," said the sage with a mischievous smile. "If it is your personal self or ego, you will never be satisfied. If it is your True Self, you will always be pleased."

"Your True Self?" asked the confused student.

"The *Self* of all of existence is the *Self* that sees through the eyes of love, even in the midst of enemies. It is the *Self* that does not judge and the *Self* that sees God in the eyes of the other. This is the *Self* that you were before your physical experience, and this is the same *Self* you will return to after your physical experience.

The sage continued, "The little gear or your personal self cannot turn the big gear of your True Self. However, the big gear can turn the little gear, and all motion becomes effortless. As you love, you become the big gear and allow all the other smaller gears of life to move with the motion of love."

"When you feel full of *Self* is when you are full of Love. It cannot be contained. Service is a way to share *Self* and magnify the energy of love. Are you starting to understand?" asked the sage.

"Yes. Yes," said the student confidently. "I have decided I want to be Selfish."

The sage gazed into the student's eyes, and the energy of the room suddenly shifted. The student was lost in the timeless gaze, and the sage spoke with his eyes only:

All you have to do is love, my son ... just love

You are All
Including everything and nothing
The internal compass points to every direction

Something
is the result of the focus you choose
However
everything still exists
including nothing

To experience something
You must find it in yourself
Then it will pop out from the backdrop of everything
sitting on the foundation of nothing

Everything is within *All That Is*
Including *what was* and *will be*

Everything is not *things* floating around and
you pick them out
It is the thought's creative power to summon the energy of the
atoms to form what you wish through focus and belief

The home of everything and something is vibration

There is something you should know about everything
and that is
its essence is nothing

The image of God lies within us all
If it did not
existence would not exist

Humans are a cup of God
An expression only
not the totality

If the Totality of God was experienced
we would explode from all the possibilities
entering at the same moment
We would not exist

However
through existence a glimpse of Totality can be known

A daisy is a cup of nature
It follows the laws of nature
It is not all of nature
However
within the flower
all of nature can be experienced

A small sip of the ocean
allows for the taste of the entire ocean

Taste the Essence of your *Sacred Cup* and
know the flow of its *Source*

Drink and be merry

What is a perfect life?
Is it getting everything wished for?
Is it having all the love yearned for?
Is it all the money dreamed of?
Is it the body of health and strength imagined?
Then what?

If all your meals were placed on a table
and you attempted to eat them all in one sitting
you would have a painful stomachache
Spewing all the contents on the floor
and feeling disgusted by the mess

A perfect life is not designed to be all that
all at once

The fun is in the savoring of each *meal of desire*
and allowing the flavors to fill your being
And at the same time
anticipating the excitement for the next *course of desire*

A perfect life is a life of entirety
in its incompleteness
at all times

The rose is perfect as a bud
as it is in the full bloom
Perfection is not the finite outcome
It is the delightful whole experience of the Becoming

A Portal is the entrance into the infinite

Attention is the first step to enter the gateway
between the real and unreal
It is separated by a very slim gate
some call a veil

A slight push of *yearning to know*
is all that is required to get a peek

The gate
gives an impression of being large
heavy and thick
Not even a tractor can move it
It has been forming from the time beginning

The immovable gate resembles a monster hiding in the dark
When the light is turned on
the monster is nowhere to be found

The lock on the gate
requires a special combination of Allowing
It is not a secret

A slight blow of breath can move it
to get a glimpse of Light from the other side

And when the Light is on
the gate is nowhere to be found

Accept the *Invitation* to the greatest celebration

It is a loving request for your presence to this sacred occasion

It is an open invitation to attend anytime
The best time is all the time

The message gives directions from any location
A sacred and personal GPS
Navigating and positioning

It always delivers and does not distinguish
Earning or justifying is not a requirement

The crowd awaits your Arrival
They know you well

The celebration is in your honor

After you accept
all of existence from the ants to the stars will cheer

⌒⌒

It is hiding in plain sight

The secret of your Story

The unfolding of nature
is a reflection of the unfolding of you

The journey is hidden in the seed
The flower's soul
The Story becomes exposed as it grows in the expression
of a blossom

It is in a state of continuous Becoming

You want to know the secret
Everybody does
Feverishly looking for the ground you are already standing on

Be aware of your surroundings
They are surrounding you
Showing you the secret of your Story

Like the flower
you are in a continuous state of unfolding
Your journey hidden within the seed of Soul
It could only be known by rooting in the Now
and expanding the sacred avenue of your Becoming

Observe your partners of nature
They are handing you
your Story on a silver platter

⌒⌖⌒

What course are you serving?

We are all serving Eternal Source
which allows us to give in its Name

An unending flow of expression
that pops into the illusion of life
Like the great geysers of the world
gushing to make known the origin of its fountain

If flowers and trees did not pop
nature would not be known

If stars and planets did not pop
universe would not be known

If animals did not pop
body's intelligence would not be known

If the sun did not pop
light and heat would not be known

If mountains did not pop
Earth would not be known

If you did not pop
God would not be known

Be the Fountain of Eternal Source
to serve the ultimate course

As you look into another's eyes
It is You looking back at You

This is the Great Awakening
The knowledge of Oneness that the ancients and the mystics
passed down

The life force is the same in all
Animate and inanimate
Whether it be a human or animal
plant or rock
Just different expressions of the Divine

The flute player blows the breath into the instrument
and different notes are heard
It is the same breath
just different expressions of sound

With this insight
allow separateness to dissolve

And free the Eternal Life Force
that is You

Embrace yourself
through loving the other

A SACRED MOMENT ON
SERVICE

Service is when you give of yourself. It can be expressed in the giving of time, money, or your full attention. What self are you giving? Pure service is when you give of your True Self from the place of love.

To serve is not helping people, animals, nature, or whatever you choose. This implies a *lack of* on the part of the serviced. To serve is to remind the other of their Greater Self: their True Self. For this to occur, your service must be in alignment with Eternal Source. When in this state, you are filled will love which cannot be contained; it overflows. It is only released by giving and serving, an endless reservoir with a returning motion.

MEDITATION

Gently close your eyes and bring awareness to your breath; inhale and exhale slowly for three cycles. Picture in your mind's eye the service you perform each day: watering the plants, feeding your pets, cleaning the house, and caring for your family and friends.

Next, bring your attention to how you are served: through *That* which moves your breath and heartbeat, through *That* which allows you to see, hear, smell, feel and taste—how the Life Force gives of itself with no asking in return, just gives for the sake of love. This is true service.

Now shift your attention to the present moment and say to yourself, *Be still and know I AM.* Sit in silence and allow the statement to resonate within you for three minutes. If thoughts enter, repeat the statement: *Be still and know I AM.*

After the three minutes, slowly open your eyes and continue the day or evening, with gratitude for being served and awaiting the opportunity to serve.

❦

6

❧

Don't See and You Will See All

True Seeing is without eyes

If the eyes of the world are your main source of sight
you see what you know
That's all

If the eyes of Spirit are your main source of sight
you see what you don't know
And that's all there is

When you see what you know
you really don't see at all

When you see what you don't know
you See what *was*
is and *always will be*

And how do you see what you don't know?

With the *Eye of Heart and Soul*

By feeling the Feeling behind all feeling
By seeing the Seeing behind all seeing
By hearing the Hearing behind all hearing
and on and on and on

What is it behind all seeing
hearing and feeling?

It is Love
It is always Love

⌒⊙⌒

When looking
all you will find is
what's not there

You look for this and you look for that
And continue to look and say
That's not it
That's not it either

When looking for something in particular
you are not allowing the Process to do its process

Looking has the emphasis on the outer world
What you are looking for cannot be found in the outer world

When looking
you are closed to allowing
All That Is

You see
by looking
it will never be found

By allowing
It will find you

We search and search
What is it that wants to be seen?

It cannot be seen with your eyes
You've tried so many times
Your eyes do not see

See past the seeing you think you see

Beyond time and space
between thoughts
between breath
between action

within silence
within depth
within presence

This is where you reside
In the *Unseen*
And this is what wants to be seen
Search no more

Seeing is seen in the
Unseen

To be whole
we seek the missing parts in the other
The other cannot provide the missing parts

Can you use a piece of one puzzle to complete another?

All the other can do is offer a hint

The focus has *a returning motion* if the piece is to fit
It is the way of the *Tao*

When looking to another to feel whole
ask the question
Where are you to be found?

Certainly not in the other

Now think
Where are you to be found?

∽

What do we do with all the injustice?
It doesn't seem fair

Some get fatter at the expense of the ones giving all
leaving them with only skin on their bones
What can be done?

The world is made by frequencies of beliefs

As long as we see injustice
injustice will prevail
The dichotomy will always exist
It is how the world operates
However
the resonance scale of the *frequency of belief* can be risen

It can result from what the highest *frequency of belief* once was
is now the lowest *frequency of belief*
Bringing the whole resonance scale to new heights

If the highest resonance is having *little food* in the refrigerator
and the lowest is *not having any food* in your refrigerator
raise the resonance scale

To raise the resonance is not to continue
falling victim to old frequency belief patterns

And the highest can be a refrigerator *filled with food*
and the lowest is having *little food*
Not having any food no longer exists
It is not on the scale

The frequency shifted from what was highest
is now the lowest

There is no ceiling for the resonance scale
There will always be highest and lowest
Which highest and lowest will you choose?

It requires an adjustment of your beliefs
and assuming responsibility for the part you play
Place the power where it belongs
Within you

Contrast of duality in the physical world will always exist
Do not give the power to the fat ones and allow them to chew
on your bones

Operate from the Highest Perspective
The severity of injustice will loosen for you

There is a Divine Design within every aspect of life
The blueprint is in you

Injustice allows justice to sharpen
and reveal what you really want

Without contrast
the picture cannot be seen

Can you imagine a painting of only one color?

Acknowledge
the *One* who sees *through* your eyes
not the one who *interprets from* your eyes

There is a difference

The *One* who sees *through* your eyes
is not the you
you think you know
It is the You
you are
The connection to Love
The capacity to view from an extensive perspective

When you interpret from your eyes
you are seeing a false representation
A murky illusion
with no depth

When you see *through* your eyes
Origin and Destiny
and everything in between becomes clear

⌒⌒

SACRED CONVERSATION

Question: How important are beliefs?
Answer: You *see through the lenses of belief*
               Beliefs are so strong they crystallize and harden
               to mold the world

Question: How do I know what I believe?
Answer: *Look at your world*

⤸

TIP YOUR HAT

A man needed a hat for the celebration of the year. He went into the town store and said to the clerk, "Show me the best hats in the store. I need to look fantastic and better than everyone else at the celebration." As the clerk went to fetch the hats, the man whispered under his breath, "I'll show them."

The clerk said, "Here are my best." The first hat the clerk pulled out was a shiny black top hat.

The man put it on his head and looked in the mirror. He adjusted the hat a few times and said, "No, this will not do. I do not look good." And he quickly turned away, hiding his face.

The clerk pulled out another hat; a grey soft wool fedora.

The man put it on his head and looked in the mirror. He adjusted the hat a few times and said, "No, this will not do. I do not look good." And he quickly turned away, hiding his face.

This went on for a few hours, from trying on Panama dress hats, berets, Italian ivy caps, safari hats, and even cowboy hats. His response was the same, "No, this will not do. I do not look good." And he quickly turned away, hiding his face each time.

The man became infuriated and barked at the clerk, "It must be the mirror! There is something wrong with your mirror. Yes, that is it."

"I assure you there is nothing wrong with the mirror. It is just an ordinary mirror!" cried the clerk.

"I demand a new mirror!"

So the clerk brought out two other mirrors, and again, the same reaction.

"It is not me, it is the mirror. I do not look like that!" screamed the man.

The patient clerk continued to say, "I have a very special hat

... wait. I will be right back." He came out with an unusual hat and placed it gently on the table.

"This is the stupidest hat I ever saw," said the man. "Are you trying to insult me?"

The hat was black with a red ribbon tied loosely around the crown. The rims curled upward and the top of the hat came to a slight point. It looked similar to a wizard's hat.

"I am not putting that thing on. I will be the laughing stock of the celebration. All the town's people hate me, and this would be a good excuse to make fun of me. They are all jerks. The whole world is crazy, including you. I do not know what is wrong with this world anymore."

The clerk said, "Just try it."

The man put the hat on his head and adjusted it a few times. He felt different, not sure why, but just different.

The clerk had a soft, yet intense, look in his eyes and words flowed from his mouth:

See from the perspective of the Observer
It is the perspective without judging and labeling
In the absence of judging and labeling
the true essence of what it is
is experienced
And what is experienced?
It is the extension of your True Self

All the mirror does is reflect
There is nothing wrong with the mirror
All the world does is reflect
There is nothing wrong with the world

When you *see one tree bigger than another*
all you *see is the size*
When you *judge if a girl is prettier than her friend*
all you *see are physical features*
When you *like someone better than the other*
all you *see is the dislike for the other*

This is the world of duality
the world of opposites
If there is an up
there must be a down
If there is a left
there must be a right
If there is light
there must be dark
And so on

The world of duality is the dense home of the physicality
of your *Being*
It is not your *true home*
It is necessary to acknowledge the difference
This will enable you *to have fun in the playing Field*

When you *judge and label and believe it to be so*
separateness exists
This is the space where pain and discomfort live
Don't look to the world and circumstance to define you

You *define the world*
You *define the image*

Interact with the physical world as a chamber of mirrors
All reflecting you
Then you are faced with yourself
no matter what is in front of you
This is the power of creation
No need to change the reflection in the mirrors
to match your desires or wishes
It is a waste of time and is impossible to do

You cannot put a hat on a mirror and expect it to be on you

No need to be afraid of the reflection
It is you
The same is true with the world and your circumstances

Put the hat on that you prefer to wear
and the mirrors of the world will reflect that image
Look at your reflection
and tip your hat in honor of this revelation

The man looked in the mirror and tipped his hat and said, "I'll buy it."

Later that night, the man wore the wizard hat with pride and confidence at the celebration. He felt special. The town's people surrounded him and admired the hat. And for the first time, the town's people invited the man to join them for a drink.

⌇

See the *Unseen* once
and the insight will remain embedded
in your internal sight for always
If you see a flower and suddenly go blind
the image of the flower will remain with you always
True seeing is beyond the eyes of thought

As you look at the sky
it appears to be a blue ceiling covering the Earth
Actually
it is neither a color nor finite
As you look in the mirror
you appear to be standing in front of the mirror
observing your face
Actually
You have neither attributes nor location

Take the mask off and allow the endless space
to expose your true nature
The nature of *All That Is*

All That Is
is
colorless and attributeless
infinite and ambiguous
oneness and omnipresent
Yet it holds all
colors and attributes
boundaries and identities
diversities and locations
This is the paradox of the divine interaction of creation

❦

When I get an insight
I say
Oh! I see

When a problem is solved
I say
Oh! I see

When another is expressing
an opposing view and it is finally understood
I say
Oh! I see

Where is it seen?
Not through my physical eyes

The scenery remains the same
It is as though I have another eye somewhere

I rub *between my eyebrows*
to answer this perplexing question
Where is it seen?

I smile and say
Oh! I See

༄

The first time mountain is met
immensity moves you
The first time mountain is met
power overwhelms you

The *mountain-ness* is felt
through feeling

Through feeling
it is experienced
A direct perception that cannot be explained in words
Yet
an internal shift has occurred

The experience becomes part of the body
called embodiment
Embodiment is the merging of knowledge
and the essence of what allows life to be alive

There is a tendency to box the event
into a label called *the mountain*
This experience then becomes a thought
Lost within the sea of other thoughts
No distinction
No depth

Experience is a whole event by being in the present
Thought is a fragmented event thinking from the past or future

Move out of the way

Only experience makes it known
No matter what it is
From the mundane to the spectacular

Experience your life
Life will then become an experience

⌘

There are two fields of vision
Individual and Universal

Individual sight sees the universe from the individual eye
The world of duality
The world of separateness
The world of personal perspective

Individual sight sees the individual in all
Nothing more

Universal sight sees the individual through the universal eye
The world of oneness
The world of inclusion
The world of Love's perspective

Universal sight sees the universe in all
Nothing less

Life's constant change makes it predictable
It is the Law
Change from outside is fruitless
One cannot change change
Change cannot be isolated
then it would be unchanged

It occurs through the occurrence
Your life is the image of perception
waiting for the direction of change
It does not have the ability to change itself

Change is the shift of awareness
A shift from *what it was*
to *what it is*
and *what it will become*
Logically
when a change occurs
the object or circumstance appears to change
Actually
the perception changes within the perceiver's Eye
and is felt within the perceiver's body
This is the knowledge of the hidden scrolls

Go within
beyond the thought realm to adjust your vision
The Law must be felt to be Seen
To think logically and reasonably
one knows concepts
To feel
one knows life

When you notice something you do not like
or
something you do like
who is noticing the preference?

If it is you that is doing the doing
who is observing the action?

Touch this aspect
like a lucid dream
You will not only be the observer
but you will be the observed as well

The veil is lifted
A melding occurs
Now neither the observer nor the observed is present

You cannot stay in this state for too long
for there is no you

Zoom back to your life with this
Secret in your pocket

You will not be able to explain it to anyone

Yet
everyone will know
you know

SACRED MOMENT ON
SEEING

What do you really see? When you get an idea or have a realization, you say, "Oh! I see." This type of seeing is not from the eyes. So where do you really see? Believe it or not, the same applies when seeing physical manifestations.

When you see a tree or rock, where are you seeing it? Not in the eyes. The eyes are only windows. The brain and mind sets up the image. The image is seen within. What you are seeing is your interpretation of the physical experience.

When you truly See, you are in alignment with the before, during, and after; the flux of time dissolves. And the whole picture within the matrix of life is exposed. Also, the momentum of belief produces circumstance and reveals the illusion of the real in reality. The third eye is the only *Sight* to be *Seen;* everything experienced are expressions of Eternal Source in the name of Love.

MEDITATION

Take a few deep inhalations and exhalations until you feel settled. Light a candle and gaze at the flame for about a minute or two. Do not stare or strain; just gaze with relaxed eyes. Next, close your eyes and bring your inner focus to the area between your eyebrows. You may see the image of the flame, blobs of light, color, or darkness. Gently focus in that area, the portal of true Seeing, the third eye. This is the eye of intuition, the bridge between you and Eternal Source. Remain focused in this area for a minute or two.

Next, relax your eyes (still closed) and stay in silence for a few moments. Gently open your eyes and continue the day or evening with the sight of Eternal Source, in the state of Oneness and Love.

～⚮～

7

⚜

THE MOON CALLS AND I HOWL
IN RECOGNITION OF MYSELF

*The most important Voice you will ever hear
does not use words*

Listen closely
All is Calling
Observe closely
All is Calling

The flower opens
You smell it
The moon glows
You look up
The bird sings
You stop and listen
The allure of the candle's flame and
the look in another's eye
So quiet
yet
loud enough that it cannot be ignored

Listen and observe with full attention
Listen with your whole body and your whole body will hear
The Calling is heard not by the ears
The Calling is known not through thoughts
Familiar and a mystery
The drawing continues
The wonder continues
The Calling continues
You follow it and know not what it is
Or do you?
Get close
The closer you allow
Familiarity transforms into Recognition
You see
the *Calling* is from You

❦

Listen to the one Voice
There is no other

It is neither the voice of authority
nor what is right or wrong
It is neither the voice of the masses
nor the one of fear or anger

It is the voiceless Voice

Its presence is always known
But it is up to you to turn to it

It is the voice of true feelings
It is the one of truth

Once you
the listener
learns to listen
all the other voices will not be heard

⌒⟋

See what is
not what you want it to be
not what you think it to be
By seeing *what is*
you will see *what was* and *what will be*

When face-to-face with the other
whether it be flower
frog or human
let them tell their story

Listen with the *Heart's Eye*
no judgments
no preconceptions

The language of the Heart cannot be spoken

Yet
you will know what has been said
and what has been forgotten

⚊⚊

Right or wrong
Who is to say?

One may say
it is definitely wrong to kill
However
in war it is celebrated

What if someone was to harm your child?
Do you just stand by?

Right and wrong are man-made morals
and do not fit with Eternal Law

Man's attempt for order and control
uses morals as an interpretation of Eternal Law

Morals give rise to confusion by trying to distinguish
what is *in accordance with Eternal Law*
and what is *not in accordance with Eternal Law*

Eternal Law is in the present moment only

The Eternal Law is inconsistently consistent and
universally individual
Consciousness and awareness enables one to know the Law
A Law that does not have to be written down
A Law that is spoken through Heart
and understood by all

Right and wrong is the voice of Man
The absence of right and wrong is the Voice of God

Singular is in the midst of plural
Within the environment of unconsciousness
consciousness lives
Unconditional love is the only quench for the thirst
that conditional love seeks

Focus of your desire is imperative
Inform yourselves of your intention

The self who wants to
and the one who doesn't
The self who loves to run in the wind
and the one who must do the chores first
The self ready to fly
and the one who says
Stop! You'll *get hurt*

We have many selves

The lover and friend
The sister and brother
The father and mother
The courageous and meek
The adventurous and cautious

Only one wears the crown

Gather the selves and come to an agreement
Set purpose in motion
Selves will align and surrender
in celebration of the emergence of the One

⤚

SACRED CONVERSATION

Question: How do I hear my Inner Voice? Sometimes it is
not loud enough to be heard.

Answer: *It is not heard because the continuous chatter of
the ego's internal dialogue does not stop talking
long enough to hear its Call*

Your life is the experience of yourself
You are the creator of that experience

Show up for the event
You are the only critic
It is a grand production with you as the full-time director

When Soul wants to speak
step aside

All expressions are expressing Eternal Source

True communication is not from thoughts

Thoughts are the afterthought of the experience
They perceive
Not conceive

The constant message that funnels is always the same

In every experience
you *are experiencing the same Experience*

A longing to be Home
A longing to be who you are
A longing for peace
bliss and love

Wandering in this endless dream called life

The more you search in this world for meaning
the more the longings increase to an intensity called pain

It is time to long no more

Awake
You are not of this world

⚭

MORNING SKY

A child was sitting on a mountaintop, admiring the sky at dawn. The colors were so vivid: red, orange, yellow, and even purple swirling over the horizon.

"I never saw the sky like this," said the child quietly. "I want grandfather to see!" He ran down the hill and got his grandfather, who was cleaning the stables. "Come Papa, I have something to show you." All excited he grabbed his grandfather's hand and walked briskly up the hill. The grandfather was laughing and stumbling the whole way.

By the time they reached the top, the sky was different. The shades of blue and the swirling of red and purple were gone ... all gone.

"What happened?" cried the child.

The grandfather said, "Maybe another day."

The child watched the sky every day for weeks. It was never the same. And each day, even though the sky had its own unique beauty, the child did not see it because he was looking for something different.

Just when he was about to give up, it happened again. It was a little different, but still incredible, with splashes of so many colors. He ran to get his grandfather again and, of course, by the time they went up the hill, the sky changed. The boy was very disappointed.

Finally, the grandfather said, "The magnificence of the sky, like the magnificence of life, does not last too long. This is the reason why you need to enjoy it in the moment. It was for you and for you only. Maybe one day I can share it with you, but every time you come down the hill, you are missing out on the moment designed for you."

The boy thought about what his grandfather said to him. It then became a ritual for the young boy to sit and watch the sky at dawn every day before his chores. But now he observed without expectation or distraction.

He just sat and admired the sky and appreciated the experience. He realized the sky was beautiful every day in its own unique way. The boy did not compare or judge the morning skies anymore. Now, the child sat and enjoyed the sky no matter what it looked like. He saw the beauty of sky being sky. And if the colors come again, like life itself, he knew it was for the moment only and to embrace its gift during its short visit.

∽ઠ૦

Look all around

Self or essence of life is staring at you
It is in the leaf of a plant
a star
the palm of your hand

Speaking in the language of true beauty and silence
Which only you*rSelf* or Inner Being can hear

To give life attention
you are giving you*rSelf*
making life's essence known

In return It gives *ItSelf*
making your essence known

When this transaction of *Self* occurs
you may laugh when you realize
neither was taken nor given

⚬

You are the only one who knows

Why go to another?
The other cannot hold the key
that unlocks your secrets

All the other can do is to remind you
that you are the keeper as well as the locksmith

◦Ꮟ◦

Creation is the product of focus
Directed attention

Focus is the point of convergence
The axis of clarity

Expectation and result merge on the laser of focus
Result is the manifested form of expectation

Look at your results then you will know what you expected

The formula is simple

Be what you *want*
And what you *want will Be*

The story of the hundredth monkey
concerns itself with contagious consciousness

When the hundredth monkey on an island
expanded consciously to benefit itself
by washing the sand off potatoes in water
all the other monkeys on the island followed suit

Without direct communication or contact
monkeys on different islands did the same thing
Amazing

When a different belief reaches a critical point
in mass consciousness
it tips the scale and a Shift occurs
A Shift that changes the mindscape of the One Mind
Oceans and mountains are not barriers

Be the hundredth monkey
To make a ripple in this world
Non-action far exceeds action

If there is anything you can do
become conscious
By being conscious you enable other Souls to realize ItSelf

When emerged in the stream of consciousness
action becomes an effortless energy with a mind of its own
The body does without doing
Yet
nothing is left undone

Sitting on the steps of the temple

Waiting for the door to open

At first
standing
now sitting

The wait is so long
day after day
month after month
year after year

There must be someone in the temple
Why don't they open the door?

Sitting and waiting once again
not realizing the small sign next to the door stating:

Please enter

SACRED MOMENT ON CALLING

There is a constant beckoning for your presence that brings your attention to the present moment. This *Calling* is felt very strongly when you are in conflict or contrast. If you are agitated, the *Calling* is beckoning you to align with peace. If you are in fear, the *Calling* is beckoning you to align with love. When you listen to the *Calling*, within silence and stillness, you will know what has been said and remember what has been forgotten.

MEDITATION

Inhale and exhale slowly for three cycles. Gently close your eyes and breathe normally and watch your thoughts: no judgments, just observe as though the thoughts are clouds in the sky drifting by. Let them pass by with no attachment. If you hop on one of the clouds of thought and you become distracted, gently go back to watching them again.

The thoughts are telling you that they are very important. You must tell them what is important or not. Right now just observe. The part that is watching is where the *Calling* originates. Continue this process of witnessing your thoughts without attachment for three to five minutes. Slowly open your eyes and continue the day as the Observer, *in it* but not *of it*.

8

YIKES!
I'M GOING TO JUMP

Stand on the cliff of possibilities
Looking down
drop your dream and allow the Web to catch it

Yikes! I'm going to jump into my dreams
Are they strong enough to hold me?
They seem so thin at times
I'll fall right through

I've been standing on the ground of logic and condition
It's held me fine
I know what to do and what is expected
It appears safe

However
the cost of this safety is putting aside my deep feelings
I abide by the rules but forfeit my freedom
I'm in a prison
Yet
I am innocent

Would I rather sit in this cell than expose the injustice?
No! I no longer want to be incarcerated

Yes
I am ready to jump

And if this dream can't hold me
I know another one will

⤸⤸

A difficult decision had to be made
and the fear of doubt riddled my mind that night

I had a lucid dream

I was flying high over the city
Witnessing my life from a high altitude
Which I thought was not possible

Floating higher and higher
The city buildings disappearing

The sky and landscape
like I've never seen before

An expansive view that included everything and nothing
An unknown familiarity

Ecstatic from the height and not wanting to return

Nagging thoughts that the return is necessary
But how do I get down?

Flash of Insight

Now that I've seen the beauty
it doesn't matter if I fall

CSGP

SACRED CONVERSATION

Question: How do I know how to follow my dreams?

Answer: *Go with what you truly feel*
Rooted in love for yourself
and the passion of Soul
Not driven by fear or anger
Not driven by how much agreement you get
from others

∽≎∾

One step closer to your dreams
is
one step closer to you*rSelf*

Dreams are the map
Desires are the signposts leading to your true Residence

Follow the circular motion
Become teachable

Fulfill your dreams

Within them is the center view of 360 degrees

A Time comes in one's life
when all you thought was real is an illusion
All you stood for falls
All you believed is untrue
All you felt was important is irrelevant
All the time you thought you had is gone

Swimming in a sea of choices and possibilities
that seem to surface along with the
Awesome Responsibility

The responsibility to live a life with love and passion
A life that is living

A time comes in one's life
to choose a life between living or dying
while in this body

⌒⌒⌒

Mind is searching for the proof of beliefs
Dream is searching for itself

Mind will zoom in to confirm
Dreams will expand to allow

Mind is from logic
Dream is from passion
Mind is from brain
Dream is from Soul

When mind is zooming in
all the rest is lost
Focus is on the particular
The particular is all that is seen

When zooming in on a leaf
the tree is lost
When zooming in on a petal
the flower is lost

As the leaf needs the tree
and the tree needs the leaf
As the petal needs the flower
and the flower needs the petal
Mind needs dream
and dream needs mind

Mind and dream in collaboration
is the formula for creation

⌒⌒

With a conscious life
responsibility follows

With a responsible life
consciousness follows

Each moment presents the opportunity of responding
to your life's experience as a projection from you

A conscious life is aware of this

A responsible life knows
Each decision
Each choice
Each thought
Each belief
Each focus
is what creates circumstance

A responsible life
consciously creates a life lived
It sets the sails
and allows the winds of the dreams to lead

Knowing
the power of creation is within dreaming

⌒⌒

Your intention adjusts the direction to complete the cycle
If you are getting what you don't think you want
look deeply

Attention will surface the intention
that is adjusting the direction
Honesty and truth must prevail

Lift the veil of ignorance
and reveal the knowledge of empowerment
There is no outside force

Whatever signals you transmit
are what you receive
Thus
circumstantial experience

Fine-tune your frequency to pick up the signals you really desire

When in alignment with your frequency
Immediately
desire
intention and experience become One

DANCING IN THE FIELDS

There was a student staring out the window of her classroom as the teacher lectured about something. She thought it was about the Civil War or civil rights, revolution or evolution. "Who cares," she thought to herself. "I hate this boring class."

As she looked out the window, she saw birds flying, the sun shining, and trees swaying. It made her feel good, and she started dreaming about becoming a dancer. She loved to dance. She danced to all kinds of music. She even danced to the sound of the wind and the songs of the birds. As she gazed out of the window, her imagination went to dancing in the fields and flying in the air where the laws of gravity did not apply.

Suddenly, the teacher said, "Sally! Sally! Where are you? What is the answer to the question?"

Startled and not sure of the question or the answer, Sally replied, "Yes, I agree."

The teacher, with a surprised look on her face said, "Correct! Dreaming is an important part of inventions. If the inventors could not dream, the inventions would never come to be. Everything you see: a chair, table, automobiles, all started with a thought, a desire, and a dream." The teacher glanced around the class and said, "Thanks to Sally for not paying attention but replying with a good guess, we will have an assignment tonight." All the students groaned, and the teacher had a playful smile on her face.

"Write a paragraph on what you dream about becoming." All the students smiled in relief, and the excitement in the room elevated. The students were talking about becoming lawyers, ranchers, singers, writers, football players, and teachers.

As the students were sharing their dreams, the teacher looked at Sally and said, "For not listening to me during the lesson, you have detention."

"What?" Sally exclaimed.

The teacher laughed and said, "I am only kidding. You are creating the world right here in my classroom. I want you to continue dreaming, but please not always during my lessons."

They both burst into uncontrollable laughter. And from that point on, this class became Sally's favorite.

⌒⊙⌒

Dream
The ingredients of reality

Dream is the real in reality
Reality is unreal without dreams
Know the distinction

Let the children dream
They are creating the world
If we stop them
we are forcing them to live in our nightmare

Dreams of love and peace
abundance and joy
passion and creation
create the path for others to walk on

The world's birth comes from dreaming

Each experience when approached consciously
will mold and fine-tune the following experiences

An experience is a belief
that has jumped out from you into the physicality
to be sensed

You sense the experience as your circumstance
and present it as your reality

You are the author and artist of your Living Picture
called your life
Keep what you enjoy and edit what you do not

It takes focus and desire
for the Thinker to turn from the previous non-serving thoughts
to thoughts of dream energy

The wise have the awareness of the *conscious window*
It is the ability of consciousness to look out into the world
as well as look back in
The origin of perception

Experience the experience

Then stand back and admire your piece of art

Do not worry
Your dream can never be bigger than you

Dreams are designed to make the grid
for the *state of matter* to follow
forming the material world

Your *eyes are the symbol*
for your *capacity*

You see the ocean and mountains
sun and moon
and the light of the stars
Much larger than your eye
Yet
the eye can take it all in

How is it that something so small can see the universe?

Eye
I
Is it a coincidence?

∽

Taking a leap into your dreams can be very scary
Especially
when the leap seems so far from where you are now
to where you desire to be
There seems to be so much to lose
Yet
the push is ever present

The frog has the answer

The frog in the pond can only leap when a lily pad is close by
When the frog wants to go to the other side of the pond
it leaps from lily pad to lily pad
The frog will reach its destination on the other side of the pond
by one lily pad at a time

The real leap is taking that first step or hop
Leaps are not the distance
Leaps are the commitment to start the dream of Becoming
And the rest will follow
Each lily pad represents
the satisfaction of taking the first step into your dream
Through each step the fear gradually dissolves
And
the dream becomes clearer

When the shore of the dream is reached
like the frog
you are prepared to handle it
For it was not a grand leap from where you started
just a little hop from where you are now

We cannot teach anything
we do not understand

We cannot give anything
we do not have

Most importantly

We cannot dream anything
that is not already existing

How wonderful is this?

⁓

SACRED MOMENT ON
DREAMING

We were told as youngsters in school to stop daydreaming. The adults did not realize that the youngsters were creating the world. Conscious dreaming, day or night, is about the Becoming; this is part of the creation process. Everything you see in this physical world started with a thought, a desire, and a dream: a chair, car, career, relationship, computers ... a baby.

The dreamer is always dreaming about the Becoming of something more. Dreaming goes beyond the boundaries of the paradigm you are living. Dreams allow you to hitch the ride of possibilities and live the adventure of who you are.

MEDITATION

Gently close your eyes; inhale and exhale slowly for three cycles. Next, think of something you would like to change in your life to make it better or more exciting. It could be a job that will be more satisfying or a more loving relationship, better health, more peace ... whatever you think would make you happier and bring more joy into your life.

Imagine yourself in your mind's eye having that which you desire. If there is a resistant thought saying, "It cannot happen," imagine a part of the dream that has less resistance. Change the thoughts of resistance to thoughts of possibilities.

For example, if you have a dream of becoming a famous actor, you may not be ready to embrace the wholeness of the dream by having accomplished movies and notoriety. And resistant thoughts may interfere with the dreaming process. For example, thoughts saying, "You have no experience; you are too old; you are not pretty or handsome enough to be an actor." These are thoughts that you have believed in for a long time; they are quite strong.

To soften the thoughts, imagine situations of possibilities that seem reachable for now: maybe going to acting classes, reading scripts, being on stage, or receiving a telephone call for a small part in a movie. Once you find an easier dream to work with and believe in, the larger dream becomes more of a possibility. Remember ... if you can imagine or dream it, it is already becoming a part of your reality.

Stay with the vision of your desire for three minutes and *feel* what it would be like to have it in your physical reality. Slowly open your eyes and continue the day as though it already happened. Most importantly, enjoy the unfolding.

9

THE WAY TO LESS IS TO BECOME MORE

The process of Becoming is not as difficult as it seems
The complexity lies within the resistance of accepting how
simple it really is

The seed of the mighty oak falls on sacred ground
As it grows
it is always an oak
Always in the state of Becoming
Becoming more of what it is
This is growth
Life's purpose
All too often humans strive to be less
Less than what we have been

Become more of who you are
not less than who you were

The way to less is to become more
Being less angry
become more tolerant
Being less fearful
become more courageous
Being less doubtful
become more confident
Being less hateful
become more loving
See where the attention lies
more or less

The nature that governs the oak
is the same nature that governs you
It is the essence of confidence and growth
of peace and love
of intelligence and determination

You spend a lifetime striving to be these qualities
You already are these qualities

The state of Becoming is the
coming to Be

Listen closely
You *are Becoming what* you *already are*

Laughter is an intimate dance
Waltzing with your Eternal Partner
And being swept off your feet

In the moment
tears of joy rolling down your face
your stomach aches from the pain of joy
a breath is difficult to inhale

You are lost in the laughing

All Is Well

It is funny when you are lost
is when you can be found

Within every *part*
the *whole* exists
The part cannot have its own agenda
The whole allows the part to have purpose

When the fruit is grown
it is picked and the sweetness enjoyed
Within the fruit lies the seed
Within the seed lies the blueprint of the tree's dream of its
Becoming
If the whole image of the tree was not in the seed
the fruit would not exist

Like the tree
your manifestations are the fruit to enjoy the sweetness
Within your manifestation is your desire
Within your desire is the seed of Soul
Within the seed is the blueprint of your dream and your
Becoming
If the whole image of your desire was not in Soul
your manifestations would not exist

When you eat the fruit of your manifestations
you are left with the taste of the Whole
Its Origin

This is a reminder
you cannot exist without the Whole Picture
And it is your *part* to know this

A MASTER

I walked in the forest yesterday. My mind was racing, and I felt weak and confused. I continued on the path and noticed each time I crossed over the shadow of a tree, a strange feeling came over me.

I stopped in the shadow of a tree and, looking up, I realized I was standing in the shadow of a master. I began to admire the tree. Its beauty and dignity certainly owned the title of majestic. I hugged the tree's enormous trunk: strong and unshakable, its roots deep within Mother and its branches reaching for the light.

A Voice interrupted:

Allow these masters to remind you of your Magnificence
Your connection to the Earth and the Heavens
The tree
among others
is a master
When you can see and most importantly
feel its majesty
then you will know yours

If you can see the strength of tree
you will know yours
If you can see the wisdom of tree
you will know yours
If you can see the magnificence of tree
you will know yours
If it was not in you
you would not be able to see or feel it

So spend time and stand in the shadow of a master
  Let it show you about you
Then turn and see the shadow you cast upon the world

I turned as I was told with the sun on my back. And to my surprise, I was now standing in the shadow of a Master.

SACRED CONVERSATION

Question: What is the Soul?

Answer: *The Soul is the Eternal Dream*
                 dreaming of your Becoming

Take a stand
When you take a stand there is no room for doubt
This requires focus

This places you in direct alignment with your intention
And to ride the consent of its vibration

Anything other than this is resistance

Focus is a laser of concentrated connection with Eternal Source

The gates will open
Floods rushing in
You must ride the waves or you will be pulled under

Let go

Now you are joyously swimming
in the current that you set

༼⚮༽

Honor this body
It is the expression of your creation
The vehicle of knowing

You cannot see the spot you are standing on
You need to step aside

The body allows the stepping aside
It is a gift to experience the Ultimate Experience
of realizing you are not this body

In short

The body enables you to experience
that which you are not
to know
That which You are

When in dilemma
you are at the point of gridlock

You did all that you could do
You thought all that you could think
You said all that you could say

The mind repeats the same scenario
Silence and peace is alien
Anxiety fills your being
A way out seems impossible

Sit back
See the drama
Remove yourself from the chaos and noise
if only for a moment

See the dilemma alone
Separate from you
Not
that you are alone in dilemma

Being in dilemma is not the dilemma
The dilemma is not being in Being

⌒

The sun appears to be moving
Actually
the Earth is moving

The Earth finishes where it starts
and starts where it finishes
Therefore
no beginning or end

We are all expanding to our start

Like the Earth
we move in stillness in a circular motion
Circling *That* which gives us Light

So
what is a day?
It is just a turning
So
what is a life?
It is just a turning

Now ask yourself
to where are you truly moving?

When wanting gets in the way of your happiness
Know the Now is too frightening

When the wants are so intense
that you will not be happy until they manifest
your true happiness will never be reached

When desires cause pain
their purpose is lost

Happiness begins here
Even though it seems to be there

If over there looks good
bring it into here

Then you will experience what is there
Now

Innocence reveals simplicity
No intellectual realizations are needed
No complex thoughts

A squirrel quietly eats its acorn
A leaf softly floats to the ground
The cloud gently rolls by
The infant reaches for her mother

Being in simplicity
does not mean Being is simple
Quite the contrary
The world rests on and in Being
Simplicity of Being is the opening for joy and knowledge

This is your natural state
The state of well-being
It is the essence of your Beingness
It is the essence of You
Innocence lacks the knowledge of complexity
Complexity has many integrated parts
and the Whole is difficult to find
This is what brings confusion to the world

Complexity lies on the same pillow with the limited view of
the personal self
Simplicity lies on the same pillow with the expansive view of
the Greater Self

If you look at a painting very closely
all you can see are the complex strokes of the brush
and blobs of paint
It is meaningless until you step back
Now the painting reveals
the most beautiful mountain scenery ever witnessed by you
And the strokes of the brush
and blobs of paint are no longer seen

Be life's witness
and testify that the complexity of the world lies within
the simplicity of Being

꧁

Within each cell contains the information of the whole body
Within each human contains the information of all existence

Where is the whole within the part?

How does a part know the whole
when it is only a part of the whole?

Within each word contains the message
Within each message contains the Direct Communication
signaling what you want to know

Within the wanting to know
contains what is known

The part of the whole
is the whole part

You and me
The part

I AM
The Whole

When you feel that you have no time
is when time has you

This is linear living
which exists only in the mind

Time assumes there is a past
present and future
However
there is only
Now

When you have memories of the past
you are remembering them
Now
When you have dreams of the future
you are imagining them
Now

Be courageous and jump off the timeline
You will be caught

In the race of time
the only thing you are beating is yourself

We think we are going somewhere
We think we came from somewhere
Not true

When we think we have arrived
It is here
When we think we have departed
It is here

Linear movement is life's illusion
Being in the present is Life's existence

Does a flower move from one flower bed to another
in order to bloom?
The seed holds the secret
The root holds the physical
The stem reaching for the light holds the bud
The blossom is already

Existence is the unfolding in the Now

The blossom comes to Be
just by Being

⌒⌒

SACRED MOMENT ON BECOMING

The natural world is always in the state of Becoming more of what it already is. The trees are becoming more than the seed. The flowers are becoming more than the bud. The rocks are more than the dirt it once was.

Humans are part of this process as well. We are becoming more of what we already are. Our seed is within the Soul, and it is a process that cannot be detained. In the state of Becoming, the Destiny returns to its Origin, which it has been all along.

MEDITATION

Gently close your eyes; inhale and exhale slowly for five cycles. Next, inhale and hold the breath for a count of five. Slowly exhale and hold the exhale breath for the count of three. Repeat three times.

Set an intention for the day ... the seed. Then ask yourself the question: *Am I becoming more or less?* More has a forward and expansive motion, rooted in joy and love. Less has constricting and backward motion, rooted in sadness and fear.

If your desire is to be less frustrated at work, then set the intention for more tolerance. If your desire is to eat less junk food, set the intention to eat more nutritious food. Once you choose an intention, hold it in your mind's eye for a minute or two. Know that your Soul's intention is always becoming more, never less. Slowly open your eyes and listen to your Soul's guidance for the day.

10

REACH FOR THAT
WHICH IS BEHIND YOU

You are seeking That which you already are

All rises and falls

The wings of bird in flight
The sunrise and sunset
Eyes open and close
Growth and death
What is behind the rising
falls back into

The rising and falling of breath
like the waves of the ocean
Watch this breath
Hear this breath
Feel this breath

Know this breath
through *That* which moves your breath

That which moves this breath is
That which moves the Earth around the sun
and *That* which moves the ant in and out of its hole
That which moves this breath is
That which moves the wind and *That* which the trees reach for

Know *That* which moves your breath

Through knowing *That*
you will know *All of This*

The *what ifs*
encompass a large territory
As a matter of fact
an endless territory

What if it doesn't work?
What if I don't like it?
What if I am stranded?
What if I am alone?
and on and on and on

Here is a new *what if* to add to the list

What if
you put all the *what ifs* aside
You may be surprised

With all the *what ifs* aside
you will be faced with
what is

Standing in the current of Now
Flowing with the Becoming
Feelings of well-being
with a new *what if* to add to the list

What if I become my dream?

If you try to get breath from the conditioned world
you will suffocate

The breath of life comes from your passion
What you love

This gives you the space to
inhale and exhale rhythmically

There is no rhythm in the world
It is an instrument
The rhythm comes from you
The beat is you
Then the world will follow

Does a drum create its own beat?

If your *lifeline* is connected to the outside world
you will be hanging by a thread always

If your *lifeline* is connected within
you will Be always

The depths of your Being
are like the depths of the ocean

Remains silent
through the noise
Remains still
through the motion
Remains
when all else is gone

Hold on
it will disappear
Let go
it will appear

Know your breath's Home
Its birth and death

This is where you have been hiding
Right here
all along

Confusion has never been so clear
Mind racing
Immobile
Breath suspended

A hummingbird circles my head
Mind settles
Focused and amazed by this little creature
Breath resumes

Clarity has never been so transparent

How could something so small
carry a message so big?

&

SACRED CONVERSATION

Question: What is the meaning of life?

Answer: *First find the meaning of your life*
then you will know the Meaning of Life

The individual strands of a rope
are intertwined so tightly
that if you separate the strands
it will no longer be a rope
The individual strands make up the rope

The Rope of Life is made up
of all the individual meanings
From the blade of grass to the human
and from an atom to the galaxies
Meanings that are intertwined so tightly it
becomes the fiber of existence

If you separate the individual lives and meanings
existence will not exist
The individual meanings make up life

Know your strand in the Rope
You will then know the Meaning of Life

THE GURU

A young devotee asked a *sadhvi*, a holy woman, to solve his problems. The *sadhvi* said, " I cannot solve your problems ... go to your *guru*."

"Where is my *guru*?" asked the devotee.

"Right here."

"Right here? Right where?" the devotee asked, confused.

"The guru is always present. All you need to do is turn to it. It is whatever is face-to-face with you in the moment, exposing you," continued the *sadhvi*.

The devotee looked all around. "I do not see a thing. Where is this guru?"

The eyes of the *sadhvi* rolled up, and only the whites of her eyes were seen. A stillness enveloped the room and she spoke:

The guru is present
when seeing through your eyes
not from your eyes
When hearing through your ears
not from your ears
When feeling through your heart
not from your emotions
The guru is present
when looking to no one for answers
Knowing before each question is asked
the answer is always the same
If the answer is heard
your personal message will be kept private
Alignment occurs
The results are existence
knowledge and bliss

If the answer is not heard
it will be made public for others to see
Manifesting in discomfort of the body and mind
The guru is present
when a fly lands on your shoulder
Once acknowledged
Beingness recognizes Beingness
Simultaneously
exposure of the universe rushes in like a raging river
along with the confidence of staying afloat

The Great Mystery reveals itself
In that moment
face-to-face with the fly
Divinity recognizes Divinity

The devotee took a moment to contemplate. "The guru is within me," he whispered to himself. As he absorbed the knowledge and insight, he whispered to himself again, "All is within me."

He looked at the *sadhvi* and said, "So, let me understand. All is within me, and whomever and whatever I am face-to-face with, even an insect, will direct me to my guru and answer my questions."

"Yes. Yes," replied the *sadhvi*.

"Ok, you are face-to-face with me right now," he said with a naughty smile. "So, tell me how I can solve my problems," he said jokingly.

The *sadhvi* tapped the devotee lovingly on top of his head and said,"You just did."

⌒⌒

When desiring for a goal
Your reasoning is as follows:
When the goal is achieved
All That Is will be experienced
Feeling happy and satisfied
within the state of completeness

However
what will be revealed
is *All That Is*
is in the state of incompleteness once again
On its quest of desiring the next goal

All That Is can never be reached
thinking it can be achieved through a goal is absurd
How could every possibility
imagined and not imagined be attained?

The design of this physicality is to never reach *All That Is*
Desires are a
dangling carrot to experience a glimpse of the remembrance
of *what once was*
and to continue the fire of expansion
to *what will be*

It is not in the doing
It is in the *non-doing*

As crazy as it may sound
the act of doing will lead to *non-doing*
if the intention is to experience a glimpse of *All That Is*

What is this life?
We know so well
and the next moment we are drenched in doubt
What is this life?
Where the moments of the past are wisps of a dream

Our desires fuel us toward the future
Once arrived
the fire is extinguished immediately
to make way for another to be fanned

The sound of my heart beats loudly
I listen

Bringing memories of when the wisdom was once known
Death stops the illusion of permanence
Yet the flower still grows
The wind still blows
Life is not separate from itself
Holding on
the cries of pain are felt
Letting go
the joy of Assistance is felt
Life flows through the human vessel
The river a symbol
Never a consideration to stop flowing
The only permanence is change
Life can only live through change

What is this life?
It is an eternal moment
that can only exist through change

The dandelion knows more than you think

Is it just a nuisance weed with no importance?
Would the Mother of Nature give birth to something
that has no purpose?

Take the time to be with the dandelion
No judging
Just be
Its intricate system of survival reveals its modesty

It is rooted in the present
Reaching for the light
Thriving to blossom
Becoming more of what it is
Always aware of its interconnectedness

It holds the secret of creation

The elements of the dandelion
are the elements of you
Would Eternal Source give birth to you
if there was no purpose for your existence?

We are more similar than different

The dandelion's purpose is to bloom
and to bring beauty and the sweetness of early nectar
It will even find the smallest of cracks in the cement walk
to push through
Knowing the community is depending on it to bring balance

With all this knowledge and responsibility
the dandelion continues to sway in the wind and face the light
Always in the joy of its Becoming

The dandelion knows more than you think

∽

Waiting in line at the supermarket
Waiting in a traffic jam
Waiting for a phone call

Typically
these circumstances are not appreciated
They are dismissed as unimportant and are filled with anxiety

Precious time is lost

The internal engine is revving
with your foot hovering over the gas pedal
Turn the ignition off

Relax
Take a deep breath

This is an opportunity to be with *Self*
Change waiting into Being

Welcome waiting
Within the waiting lies what you have been waiting for

Exposure
Lying open
Allowing the true identity to take form

If a bud of a flower does not open
If a baby does not come out of its womb
If the chicken does not hatch
They would never be known and die holding their identity
Denying the world of their Magnificence

Exposure is the part of the life cycles
and gives diversity and beauty to be experienced
It also gives wonder and purpose
for expansion and growth

If all stayed hidden
there would be no world

Break your shell
Expose yourself

The world is expecting you

Move out of the Way

The moving out of the way is
the stepping outside of the static

Static interferes with the Message

Static is from thoughts with no direction
Building on the vibration of fear
Resulting in the *energy-wasting thoughts* of
depression and worry
anger and fear
guilt and shame
This is when thoughts lose their focal point and power

When the television has static
the picture cannot be seen
In the midst of the windstorm
nothing can enter

The focal point of power
is when thoughts are in community

Thoughts are like atoms and need community
Hydrogen and oxygen join together
to form the molecule of water
If hydrogen and oxygen did not join in community
water would not exist

When your thoughts are in community with Eternal Source
they become powerhouses of love and excitement
Thus
flowing in an ecstatic atmosphere of possibilities

To feel sadness
happiness must exist
To feel fear
love must exist

Wrap your arms around both

Take a deep breath
and know there is a place where neither exists

A landscape with no horizon
separating the Earth and sky

❧

SACRED MOMENT ON REACHING

We are reaching and striving for *That* from which we originate. The reaching is so strong and intense because we know what to expect. It has already been experienced. The reaching is the desire to experience it again.

The experience is right here, right now. However, it has been forgotten, but not totally. The dream of remembrance of how it feels is why we are relentless in reaching for it again. The question to ask is where is the reaching coming from? Once answered, the *reaching* will be reached.

MEDITATION

Gently close your eyes; inhale and exhale slowly for five cycles and put your attention on the rising and falling of the breath. Watch *That* which the breath comes from and *That* which the breath falls back into; a circular motion.

Continue to observe the movement of the breath for another six to ten cycles. Slowly open your eyes, and be observant of your breath throughout the day.

の

11

EXPOSE YOUR DESIRES
AND DESIRES WILL EXPOSE YOU

Rise up to the occasion that desire offers

The ancient texts speak of striving for a
desireless state of consciousness
However
one has to desire a desireless state
Then one is in the same predicament of desiring
no desires

Desires are Soul's beckoning
The fuel of life's motion
If a flower did not have a desire to grow
it would not bloom
If a human did not have a desire to live
birth would not exist

There is a fine line between having desires to fulfill you
which they *never* do
or
allowing desires to expose you
which they are *intended* to do

Exposing leaves an empty space within the womb of Soul
Soul's usefulness is when it is filled
Filled not by obtaining an object or circumstance
filled by the Spirit of who you are
This is the divine marriage

A desireless state does not mean not having any desires
Impossible to do

A desireless state means not seeking the desire to fulfill you
It is being in the state of fulfillment and completeness
before any desire is desired
Holding the excited anticipation of revealing Soul's dream
exposing the blueprint of your Authentic Self
And knowing when the desire manifests
you will be seeking another one immediately
Channels open
Empty yet filled

This is the desireless state spoken of by the ancient ones

When your Heart is open
your mind is open

When your Heart is open
sight is limitless

When your Heart is open
Love has a place to flow

Focus your energy from head to heart center
from fear to love energy
All thoughts of pain and anger
shame and fear
confusion and sadness
transform into acceptance and trust

The battle is over
You will be caught

Cradled in a place where every possibility is possible

Even ones that will surprise you

౼౼

The manifestations of what you want begin with desire
Formulates through imagination
and becomes real from expectancy

The force behind it all is belief
Just let go

Throw the seeds of desire into the *Wind*
Falling where they will

The growth depends on the soil of belief
and allowing the Light to push the growth

Where they land does not matter
If you grow a tomato here or there
it is still a tomato

Watch the seeds as they fly
And feel the excitement of knowing their agenda

The agenda of creating more seeds
to send into the *Wind*

Who am I?
The light and dark
Heaven and Earth
Immortal and mortal
Sun and moon
Sprit and human

Who am I?
Illusion lies in the duality
Thinking there is an up and a down

In a trance
Programmed to see separateness and things
holding their own essence
When in fact everything is the Essence of Eternal Source

I AM everything
being something
with the backdrop of nothing

❧

Watch for the shooting star in
the darkest of the dark
The dark allows the light of the star to be seen

Dark is the catalyst for desires
Desires are the catalyst for joy

The shooting star is the desire against intention
It shoots high toward the Heavens to feel alive

Let it direct you
to another shooting star
and yet another

This is what keeps life expanding

Gaze into the sky of possibilities
Aim not for the star

Just enjoy the Light it brings

⌒

When a desire rises to experience a circumstance
whether it be a lover or health
money or career
know that the circumstance is not separate from you
And all the *properties* of circumstance
are directly connected to your beliefs
The *frequency of belief* contains all the properties
of the circumstance including object and location
The *object*
circumstance and location are in one bundle
They are not separate entities

If you take an object and put it here or there
it is not same object that you moved from one place to another
They are different
To place an object in a different location
requires a different perspective
A perspective is a *frequency of belief* and thought
Therefore
a different location requires a different perspective
Resulting in a different circumstance
which includes object and location

Location is the property of the object
Not that the object is the property of location
Circumstance is all inclusive and is the property of both
Contemplate this

Everything in your field of circumstance
is an extension of perception
stemming from belief

The alchemists know the *Seer*
Seeing and *Seen* are not separate
They also know *circumstance*
object and *location* are not separate

This is a major shift of awareness
The craft is to know the birth of the world is from perception
The birth of perception is from belief and
the birth of belief is from you

Circumstance is in the cycle of the one
and the One is you

⁓⊱⁓

When someone tries to shed guilt or shame on you
Dodge it
Fast
It is not yours to own

It is the other's arrows of hurt
looking for a target to ease their pain of not feeling loved
Being a target will never ease the pain for the other
The other is the only one who can ease their own pain

The aim is off
The arrows of hurt need to point in the opposite direction

Facing the archer

SACRED CONVERSATION

Question: How can one be content if one has desires?

Answer: *Desires are necessary for the expansion of life*

             Desires are to propel
             Not to define and keep
             Desires are a continuous process
             Not an end result

             Desires cannot be held
             for there is nothing to hold
             Desires are to enjoy the fleeting moment
             of the completion of its arrival

             Contentment lies in knowing this

                        ⌒⌒

Read the signpost of desire carefully
It is giving you information and direction for your journey

Just before the foot is placed on the ground
The signpost is magically placed before you
to guide the next step

All happening within the moment
Yet
predetermined

The signpost leads to your desire
However
the desire placed the signpost

The fun part is the illusion of the adventure of time and space
The conscious part is the awareness of experiencing *Self*

The signpost is the direction for you to follow
You know it well

At first
it may not seem familiar
Maybe difficult to see

Take your sleeve and rub the dust off the sign

The message on the sign becomes clearer

Remembering
you wrote it

⤆⤇

Desire after desire

One is satisfied
another surfaces

A wheel turning
The center is still
Without a center the wheel is unable to turn

What are desires reaching for?
All desires
desire wholeness
which the Center offers

The wheel turns
Life turns

Each desire reaches for where it originates
Creating the illusion of linear movement

Desires spring from the Center
and circles within the Now
Eagerly awaiting to touch Center again

This is the true movement of life
A full circle

The wheel turns

❧

RED CORVETTE

Once upon a time, there were two very close friends. They grew up together in the city. They both lived in the low-income housing called the projects. They got into a little trouble, but mostly mischievous play. They were like glue. They did everything together and used to talk and dream about getting out of the city. But there was a difference between them.

One friend was always excited about his desire of being financially successful. One day a red Corvette passed by while they were hanging out in the streets. He said, "See that car? It will be mine one day."

The other boy was always doing what he thought he should do for God's work. He had a kind and generous heart. He would say, "I want to save the world." And he always felt his buddy's materialistic values and desires were so shallow.

As they got older, one friend went to live in a monastery and was helping the poor all over the world. The other became a successful businessman; he owned one of the largest corporations on the stock exchange, called Corvettes Corp. Even though the two friends followed two very different paths of life, they still kept in contact. The love between them was strong.

When they got together, the monk would preach to his friend about being closer to God. And the businessman would laugh and hug the monk.

One day as they were having lunch, the businessman pointed to a car parked in the street. It was a beautiful red Corvette. "That car is mine. It was the driving force for me to become a successful businessman and create my corporation."

The monk shook his head. "See that building? It is the largest shelter that feeds and houses the poor and homeless. This is where I service them."

"Good for you," said the businessman as he put his arm

lovingly around his friend and continued to speak, "My brother, listen with your heart, not through your judgments." The businessman's energy shifted as he softly spoke the following words:

Desires are not to be judged
It is an intimate affair between the desirer and the desired
Universally shared
If a desire is for a red Corvette or to service the poor
both are sacred and doing desire's purpose
Judging is through the mind
Guidance is through Heart and Spirit
Desire's language is designed only for the desirer
The desirer will hear clear and precise instructions
Others will hear static
Let me assure you that the cycle is in motion
Revolving around the center of Self

The monk took a moment to reflect on these words. The businessman took a breath and spoke additional words:

If one says:
Do you think the world revolves around you?
You can reply with confidence
Yes, it surely does!

The monk laughed and said, "You never changed."
They hugged and said goodbye. The monk turned and walked into the shelter not noticing the sign hanging on the wall:

"Donated by Corvette Corp"

The mind is not the home of any original ideas
As a matter of fact
it is not the home for any ideas
The mind does not have the capability
for this enormous undertaking
The mind will make an idea known
after the *infusion*

The brain is a receptor
and receives data from the higher realms of
Eternal Source

Then the mind perceives the *infusion* of inspiration
And the Soul will give direction
The choice to follow it or not is in your hands

This knowledge allows the opportunity to adjust your vibration
to become an open channel to allow new ideas

Like the farmer who gently drops the seeds into the soil
The soil does not know the outcome of the seed
until it is planted
The mind does not know the idea until it is *infused*

Rich and fertile soil is needed to activate the seed
Clear and focused mind is needed to activate the idea
Sun and water promote the seed's growth
Allowance and inspired action promote manifestation

Be mindful of this sophisticated operation
and get out of the way

Desires are the treasure map
to discover where the valuable secret is buried

The valuable secret is buried close to the surface
and holds the love and joy that impelled the desire

Manifested desires do not hold the secret
They just appear that they do

The love and joy of manifestation lasts only for a moment or two
then off again to another treasure map of desires

Desires are in quest of themselves

Where is the secret?
This is the divine comedy

Close up
it may seem like a tragedy
From far and above
it is hysterical to the wise

The wise know
what we desire
we already possess

So what's the rush?

Today starts the momentum for tomorrow

Tomorrow can be anything you want
Thus
starting the momentum today

Each morning you are born from
the night's sleep into the awakened state
Coming out of the womb into a new world
with a backdrop of yesterday

Yesterday's thoughts are nothing more than
yesterday's thoughts

But today's thoughts are thoughts of the future
filled with potential and possibilities

Yes
Today contains the momentum of anything you desire

⬤

SACRED MOMENT ON
DESIRES

Desires are the fuel of life. They are our guide for expansion. Expansion is growth. And growth allows joy, love, and happiness, creating life's flow. The problem lies in thinking the desire that comes to fruition, holds the joy, love, and happiness—not so. It is the journey of desire's becoming that brings joy, love, and happiness, not the manifestation itself.

MEDITATION

Gently close your eyes; inhale and exhale slowly for three cycles. Think of a time when you were really happy. If this is difficult, imagine what it would be like to be happy: feelings of contentment, lightheartedness, joy, and delight. Stay with this image in your mind's eye for a few moments.

In your mind's eye, stand in front of a mirror and look at your face: bright eyes radiant, happy, and smiling. You feel so good. Absorb and bathe in this feeling and image. Inhale and exhale three times, and know happiness is always with you. The stream of well-being never leaves.

Slowly open your eyes and for the entire day, look for happiness in yourself and others.

12

Never Will She Sleep

Surrender into Her arms

The warmth of a woman
is always from Heart
The nurturing of a woman
is always from Heart
Woman and Heart are true sisters
A woman sees from Heart
Her feelings her guide
Heart is the true connector
She knows this

Soul
represents the feminine
The space for creation
Spirit
represents the masculine
filling the space to set in motion
The melding of both
is the basis of existence

Goddess Energy has been suppressed in fear
Women representing that energy have been
suppressed in fear

Watch out!
She is arising
not only in Woman but in Man as well

The *Goddess Energy* has been awakened
Once awakened
never will she sleep again

Allow the natural movement

The Mother of nature is in the constant state of Becoming
teaching through her example

She is showing and embracing the beauty of her love

Every seed has the potential for greatness
Her instructions are clear:

We do not move into the future
We attract the future into the Now

Use your focus and vibrate to what is within your seed
Rooted in Soul
And allow the Magnificence to express itself

Tuning forks will sing together
when they are within the same frequency

Vibration calls
the desired to its Home

Be the tuning fork you are meant to be
and attract the harmony of your creation

Goddess Energy has surfaced
It is the energy of passion

The *Goddess Energy* is the missing part
from the false interpretation of God

God has been fragmented
Humans are fragmented

God and Goddess are one
Expressing the love energy of unity
It is time for the divine marriage
To embrace each other in the wedding dance

The imbalance occurs when only one is recognized

You cannot have one without the other
in the world of duality

When the vows are taken
each dissolves into one another and becomes indistinguishable

⤶

Sisters of Spirit

When we gather
we dance in the Light
we sing in the Light
we laugh in the Light

The ramp is lowered
and access inside the fortress is available

The feminine energy swirls around and through
And carries us on the
wave of intensification and intoxication

As we ride the wave
collectively we are One

Within the One
individually we are *All That Is*

Oh Yes!
Hail to my
Sisters of Spirit

PERFECT

A mother and son were eating dinner in the sunset's quiet. Her son asked abruptly, "Am I not the best?"

"You certainly are," said the mother.

"Am I not the most wonderful?" he continued.

"Yes. Yes, you are," she replied.

"Am I the most perfect?" shouting in his loudest voice.

"Yes!" the mother shouted back.

"No, I'm not. I don't do everything right," the son said sharply.

Lovingly and calmly the mother began to explain. "Even the so-called mistakes or learning moments, my dear son, are perfect for where you are. Perfection does not mean you do everything right; no such perfection exists."

The mother proceeded to pick up a delicate plant that was on the windowsill. The plant had both buds and blossoms on its stem. "Is the bud perfect?" asked the mother.

The boy examined it closely and spoke confidently, "Yes, it is."

"Is the blossom perfect?"

After he examined it again, he replied, "Yes."

"Is one more perfect than the other?" she continued.

"No," the child said with a thoughtful look on his face. "You can't compare them," continued the boy.

She looked into her sons eyes and said, "Remember this!"

There was a pause. Then the son smiled in acknowledgment. He touched the plant's soil and said, "It needs water. I'll water it."

"Perfect!" exclaimed the mother

The future of your dreams exists now
Waiting to be allowed to enter

The pull of the future self
uses the passion of desire as bait

In order for desire to be bait
it has to have a strong belief of the catch and a line of allowing

Use the bait
and the fish is caught

Do not use the bait
and you will be sitting endlessly in the dingy
wondering why you are not catching any fish

Look
under the surface of the water
The hook is dangling
The line is intact

But
where is the bait?

SACRED CONVERSATION

Question: Religions always refer to God as *he.*
                Is God a he or she?

Answer: *God's attributes are All That Is*
                and All That Is Not

                Soul represents the feminine
                Spirit the masculine
                Either would not exist without the other
                They are expressions of one and the Same
                The other defines the other
                only in the world of duality

                God is not dual
                God is inclusive.

                Religions like to label and separate
                It is just a fumbled attempt
                to control and restrict the feminine energy
                and block the whole experience

                God is
                      he and she
                            both and neither

Be the mother of your thoughts
They are your children
They are the cradle of your creations
and have stayed with you as children do
How long should they stay?

Distinguish the age of the thoughts
If they are young thoughts that never grew up
they have no direction and are running wild
If they are not pleasing to mother
it is time for them to grow up
And transform into thoughts of focus
with her loving direction and guidance
If they are mature thoughts
they have a momentum and direction of their own
If they are pleasing to the mother
there is no need to interfere

Allow them to move *through* you not *from* you
Thoughts are interpretation
in the sea of Mind
Feelings are the home of the interpretation
in the soil of body

The young thoughts have been housed long enough
Allow them to detach
And as a mother
watch and observe their play
You have given birth to them
however
you do not have to support them for life

To see who you are
acknowledge the *I* referring to the personal self
A changing phenomenon
She or he
sad or happy
young or old
likes or dislikes
Constantly unfolding and becoming vulnerable to the Light

To See who you truly are
Acknowledge the *I AM* referring to your Higher Self
An unchanging phenomenon
omnipresent and infinite
all-pervasive and divine
Constantly embracing you to become lost in the Light

∽

A compassionate mother
stands by her child who is crying over a broken toy

She comforts him
And knows from the vision of her life
the child must move through this to evolve into adulthood

One day the toy will drop importance
and this moment will be reflected on with a smile

From the vision of the Summit
like the mother
look upon the world's pain and suffering
with compassion and to comfort

Knowing we
as humans
must move through this to evolve into conscious beings

And one day
importance will shift
and the moment will be reflected on with a smile

⚮

Bring the thoughts
from head to heart center

Now the thoughts have a different perspective

When thoughts are from heart
Thinking is from heart
Therefore
utilizing the whole body not just the head

Thinking from the head
is a limited perspective

Thinking from heart
is an expansive perspective
It is in direct communication with Eternal Source

Bring the thoughts down

The brain is a receiver
The mind is a perceiver
The heart is a transceiver

The heart shares the same circuitry with Eternal Source
interpreting the sacred language
Spoken only in the Now

Align with Heart and listen

The light of the sun has no shape
It gives beauty to that which it falls upon

Spirit has the same nature
Shining in Soul
Giving it attention and light

The Soul offers the shape to be known
which the feminine contains
The shape of authenticity
The shape of desire

Let her sing
through passion
creativity and inspiration

Her tune will seem familiar
for her song is your true voice

A mother is a giver
She gives with joy
It is her nature and her purpose

A great example of mother energy
is the Mother Earth
Always in the state of giving and asking for nothing in return

Mother
does not tell the flower how to grow
She sets the motion
And allows the flower to bloom in its own expression

The flowers come *through* the mother
not *from*
Letting go is a must
The mother is the vehicle for the flower to bloom
and share with the world

The same process is with the humans
Children come *through* the mother
not *from*
Letting go is a must
The mother is a vehicle for the child to bloom
in his or her own unique expression and share with the world

❧

She speaks of the Cycle
of which she is intimately connected

The law of nature is a blessed cycle of life and death

A carrot's death is for the sake of the eater
When *death gives way to life*
it is a sacred sacrifice for life's sake
And the Cycle is in motion

Beware for there is an Anti-Cycle

An elephant is taken for ivory greed
When *life gives way to death*
The motion stops
causing chaos and confusion

Be prepared for this has great
ramifications that we must all endure

Be a giver to *Life's Cycle*

Within
lies the secret of immortality

SACRED MOMENT ON GODDESS ENERGY

Feminine energy is the necessary component for life. It is the energy of creation. The masculine and feminine energies are not separate. They are expressions of the Whole. They both are born from the force of *Source Energy,* expressing duality. Duality is needed for experience. Embracing both expressions as One is needed for enlightenment.

MEDITATION

Gently close your eyes; inhale and exhale slowly for three cycles. In your mind's eye, imagine a safe and beautiful place in nature: the forest, beach, mountains, or desert.

Look all around and feel the essence of the place. Feel the ground, the wind on your face, and the sun on your back; hear the crashing of the ocean waves, the buzzing of insects, and the songs of the birds. Smell the fragrances of flowers and taste the salt on your lips. Use all your senses in your imagination, and stay with this image for a few minutes.

The Earth is the representation of *Goddess Energy*. Sit in her palm and feel her love. Slowly open your eyes and start the day with an appreciation of Mother Earth and all she gives.

∽

13

❧

SHHH!
LISTEN

Silence is where it is heard

The Silence of silence is beyond silent
The silence of noise is the halting of sound

But what is the Silence of silence if there is no sound?
It is beyond the duality of sound and no sound

The Silence of silence is neither in time nor in space
It is recognized between the transition
of the inhalation and exhalation
It holds all
yet
all knows it not

Within its presence we squirm or allow
If we choose to squirm
the message of Silence will not be heard
If we choose to allow
the message of Silence will be known

In Silence the quiet is so loud
it is deafening

Deafening to the sound of the world
Yet
hearing *All That Is*

Within Silence
lies the basis of existence

Flakes
collectively snow
Trees
collectively forest
Sand
collectively beach
Drops of salted water
collectively ocean
Quiet
collectively silence
Moments
collectively life

Love
collectively God

◦≈◦

THE ELEVATOR AND NOISY THOUGHTS

A man stepped out of the accounting office. His tax forms were completed, and he was not happy. He was so angry and upset; his face felt like it was on fire. "Why do I have to pay taxes? This is unfair." He grumbled and complained to himself.

This man was very rich, and his accountant always suggested that he donate some money to a charity to reduce his taxes, which he never wanted to do. As the man stood in front of one of the two elevator doors, his mind raced with angry thoughts—a familiar state of mind for him. The elevator doors were on opposite sides of the hallway. He impatiently pushed the button to the elevator many times. The door did not open, "Damn," he said out loud.

He pushed the button again and again, and no door opened. Next, he slammed the button with his fist. He looked at his hand and a little trickle of blood dripped from his knuckles. "Great," he mumbled and licked the blood off his hand.

He went back to his noisy thoughts, filled with the old fears of letting go of his money and future fears of never being able to replace it. He never really knew how to feel good. He was always worried about something that could happen or depressed about what had already happened.

When he was younger, he would look for signs from God on how to feel better, but they never came to him. He grew detached, angry, and alone. He looked to the one elevator door to open, but it never opened: a familiar occurrence for him. He was always angry and distressed about something, always in the mind of noisy thoughts that clouded his vision. "Oh, I will take the stairs!" he cried.

The man was filled with noisy thoughts and focused on only one of the two elevator doors. He never noticed that every time he pushed the elevator button, the other elevator door behind him always opened ... he missed the opportunity.

All moves in silence
The true workings of life work silently
Hands write in silence
Birds fly in silence
Trees grow in silence

Listen closely
In silence everything is said
without saying anything

∽⊖∾

When the Earth is in its natural state
all is at peace

Sitting in its palm
it is natural to be natural
This is when the Earth sings silently
Yet
loud enough to be heard

When the Earth is paved with cement
trees uprooted and buildings blocking the sun
it is forced to conform to unnatural standards

On the street
it is natural to be unnatural
Peace is craved for which the cement separates

This is when the Earth cries out loud
Yet
it is not heard

SACRED CONVERSATION

Question: There are so many voices in my head. How do I
                know which one to follow?

Answer: *Follow the voice of love*

                Unfocused thoughts that listen to fear are in a
                dark windy tunnel searching for the exit door
                The flame of the candle you are holding is
                flickering making it difficult to see where you
                are going and the exit door cannot be found

                Focused thoughts that listen to love are in a
                calm and still tunnel knowing
                the exit door is near
                The flame of the candle you are holding is
                burning brightly enabling you to see the
                exit door clearly which is always
                open for you to enter

                              ∽⊖∼

Silence beneath silence is heard
Wind pushing wind is felt
Light shining light is seen
Love behind love is experienced

This is the nucleus of All that is brought into existence

The nucleus of *That* behind *This*
Setting up the forum to be known
but impossible to touch

Akin to gravity
It springs from the nucleus of the Earth
Feet on the ground proves its existence
However
to find it would be an endless search
leading to nothing and nowhere

Nothing is the reason for everything
Nowhere is the reason for everywhere

There is a world where nothing exists
yet
it is the home where everything exists

The worldless world
holding the world
It is *That* which is not
and allows the *Is*

The worldless world supports the world
The world can only be the world through being worldless

Listen to the *music of matter*
The atoms await direction from you
Vibrating out of love
Atoms are the energy of light and sound
The tone of belief's expression

Roaming aimlessly until you orchestrate the music
The world springs from vibration
It was known in the Bible
In the beginning was the Word
It was known by the yogis
Aum is the primordial sound

Thought precedes matter

Matter is vibration
Its solidity forms from the expression of beliefs
Beliefs embodied from collective and individual consciousness
Once the beliefs are manifested in the world
they are perceived by the mind and labeled reality

When you see the ocean
you are seeing the atoms playing the tone
labeled *ocean*
Same as a tree and chair
lover and you

This is your life's movie
You are the director
Beliefs are the negatives
Eternal Source is the Light

And the atoms gather in the projection
obeying the attracting force of Love to create the tone
A tone that will be experienced

And the music is beautiful

❧

The sky opens and thunder roars

The blaring roar loosens the sleepy gravel
to expose the green luminous gem
lighting the path for your first step

Thunder roars to reveal the path of freedom is love
No longer carrying the heavy load of rubble

The mind cannot resolve
It can only recognize the resolution
You cannot think your way out

Insight is from the inner realms

Clear the rubble
Offer it
Turn it over
Sit in the silence

Silence offers the dark for the spark to be seen

The gem is you
The luminosity is You
Now
Thunder roars to wake you up!

⤮

The stream of silence
enables me to hear the beat of my heart
along with the Ultimate Pulse of Being
here and not here
here and not here

In the midst of an autumn day
a leaf falls
I observe the leaf falling
being
here

In the midst of an autumn day
a leaf falls
I AM the leaf falling
being
not here

In the stream of silence the two worlds are exposed
Mortality and immortality
here and not here

The choice between the Pulse
is to ride the stream or Be the stream

It's not normal?
It's not natural?
What are you crazy?
What is wrong with you?

It is heard time and time again
from others who disagree

What is not natural is the judging
The very act these statements imply

Look at Mother Earth
Do you see a tree judge another tree
because it is smaller?
Do you see a squirrel judge a raccoon
because it looks different?
Judgments imply all flowers must be roses of one color
Look around
All is what it is
in silent Acceptance

When one hand reaches for the other
it seems to have a mind of its own

Knowing what to do and when to do it
without interference from you

The two hands clasp each other
creating a circuit of two hands becoming one

Even when separated
the hands are waving and gesturing
as though conducting some unheard music

Hands in prayer position
symbolize the two worlds becoming one
Heaven and Earth
Spirit and body

The hands are designed to hold and be filled

Yet
when the hand is ready to receive
it is always empty

⸺

Silence enables music to be heard
If it was not for the silence between the notes and tones
the vibration of sound could not be distinguished

Therefore
no music

Space of Silence is in every aspect of life
Between the inhalation and exhalation of your breath
Between steps of your walk
Between night and day
Between the blink of your eyes
Between thoughts
Between the wing's motion of a bird in flight
Between words
Between lifetimes

The home of Silence is where everything lives quietly
Embracing the most Heavenly music
not yet known to the masses

It is no wonder this is where
all the answers
all the solutions
all the ideas
are waiting patiently to greet you

Please remember

Through stillness
the motion of Spirit is felt

Through silence
the voice of Spirit is heard

SACRED MOMENT ON
SILENCE

Within silence is where all the answers are heard. How is something heard without sound? It is heard not from your ears. It is seen, not from your eyes. It is where duality does not exist. Therefore, sound or no sound does not matter. It is a placeless place where thoughts settle, the static subsides, and the underlying knowledge of *All That Is* penetrates your Being.

MEDITATION

Gently close your eyes; take a few deep inhalations and exhalations and relax for a few moments. Listen to the sounds inside your home for a moment or two, maybe the sound of the refrigerator or a clock. Next, listen to the sounds outside of your home, maybe a bird singing, a car passing by, or a dog barking.

Choose one sound outside or inside and listen with your right ear for one minute. Next, listen with your left ear for one minute. Come back to your center, continuing to listen to the sound you chose with both ears for a few more minutes.

Next, bring your attention to your breath. Once you feel your body settle, slowly open your eyes and know that Silence is with you; know Silence is always with you.

14

⁓

THE SKY IS THE LIMIT WITH NO BEGINNING MIDDLE OR END

Be what you want and what you want will Be

Look to the sky
Where is it?
Can you touch the sky?

Look to the horizon
Where is it?
Can you touch the horizon?

Look to humanity
Where is it?
Can you touch humanity?

Look to the world
Where is it?
Can you touch the world?

Look to you
Where are you?
Can you touch and find you?

Are you hiding in the brain?
In the heart?
In thoughts?
Where are you?

The sky is a concept
The horizon is a concept
Humanity is a concept
The world is a concept
And guess what?
You are also a concept

⌁

At times
feelings of sadness and aloneness
unloved and unwanted
despair and hopelessness are too much to endure

Covering your face
to block out the ugly

But the feelings return with a vengeance
Not to hurt
but to acknowledge that you are burying your gem

Fall on your knees and ask for guidance
Look up
Learn from the endless sky
How it allows the clouds to drift by without holding on
This is the message

Once received
the darkness and illusion of ugly is left behind
And what remains is the beauty of Love and Light

Diamonds are hidden in dark of the Earth's rock
When the rock is chipped away
the brilliance of diamond is revealed
Your gem is hidden in the dark
When the illusion is chipped away
the brilliance of You is revealed

It is funny how life has so much beauty hidden
in what we consider the ugly

Talk to me about the mystery of Spirit
The mystery of Spirit is indeed mysterious
Its ways profound
yet
subtle

Behind and in front of
Here and there
Everywhere and nowhere
Above and below
Both and neither
Silently loud
All in one
One is all
Universally individual
It gives through receiving
Moves within stillness and is held by letting go

In the physical world
the more security you have
the less secure you feel
The more certainty you have
the less you know
The more you hold on
the less you have
The more you try to be filled
the less you feel fulfilled

So where does it exist?

Within the unseen
Feel secure about insecurity
Be certain about uncertainty
Own nothing and have everything
Be filled by being empty

Oh yes
The ways of Spirit are truly mysterious
Be a detective on the case always

Spirit playfully alluring you
Listen and watch
Be alert and aware of the clues
The messages are in forms of inspirations and insights

Spirit's mystery cannot be solved
but it can be resolved
As it reveals Itself to you
as You

Then
the mystery remains a mystery always
You remain you always
Accepting it
Bathing in it
Loving it

SACRED CONVERSATION

Question: How do I find myself? Who am I?

Answer: *It is not easy*
              Yet it is

              When you attempt to control the uncontrollable
              When action precedes inspiration
              When the negatives of fear occupy your mind
              you are nowhere to be found

              This internal combat is so loud
              it is transmitting to the forces of the universe
              to stay out

              The forces of the universe is where
              you are found
              Whispering the answer
              within every breath
              within every breeze
              within you

              The difficult part is the letting go of your
              false beliefs and allowing
              the white flag of surrender to rise
              in the midst of your internal battle

              The easy part is you don't have to do anything

Attraction occurs no matter what is happening

Attraction is a natural phenomenon
It has no discrimination
It is a neutral force searching to complete the circuit

Attraction includes all
even distraction

Distraction diverts attention from a state of well-being
to a state of confusion

The stream of well-being and the state of confusion
are within the same stream of attraction

If your distraction is chaos
know your attraction for peace is close by
If your distraction is fear
know your attraction for love is close by
If your distraction is pain in the body
know your attraction for health is close by

Stay on course
Set the magnet of your thoughts in the direction you desire

Look to where the needle is pointing

Is that who you want to be?

Hope is endless

When pushed up against a wall and nowhere to turn
Escape seems impossible
How do you get out?

Hope

When the body is not working
When the dollars are not flowing
When loved ones are gone
When aloneness envelops you
What do you do?

Hope

Hope is the light at the end of the tunnel
Hope is endless and can be any possibility
Even ones that don't even seem possible

It is the allowing of possibilities
Void of judgment
Just trust

Through allowing of hope
the forum for relief is being set up

The atoms that were wandering aimlessly are now at attention
reacting to your signal of hope
and searching for expansive possibilities

Atoms are stronger and happier when in alignment
with the force of hope

Hope is not a false expectation
Hope is the necessary component
to align your attitude with well-being
and to light the path out of the maze of distressing thoughts

∽

Height is determined by depth
The height of a mountain is determined by the depth of distance
from ground level to its summit

If one has not touched the depths of self
the highs will not be known
To feel joy
one had traveled the road of pain
To feel liberated
one had been incarcerated
To feel God's angels
one had a rendezvous with the demons

The world of duality is where the illusion of existence exists
However
the Essence of existence is not found in duality

Once the extremes of the highs and lows are felt
the next extreme is no extreme
just Being
Extremes stretch in either direction
and return back to origin
Magnetic currents of the Earth
stretch from the South and North Poles
and return back to the Earth

The attaining of the highest degree
and falling to the lowest bottom
both lead to Origination
Know whatever extreme is experienced
it will lead Home

⚬

The time factor feeds the motion of the treadmill
You have to keep going to keep time
Nonstop and always running
The support is from the outer world
If you try to stop
you will fall off
Even when the body stops
the mind keeps going

Time becomes the enemy
Racing and trying to fit all the doings within a construct of time
That does not even exist
Therefore
it cannot be done
Time pushing against you and the discomfort pushing back
The battle begins

Be mindful
It is the opportunity to be in the timeless Now
Now is the flux of the past
present and future existing simultaneously
Time will succumb to you and become your ally
not your enemy

It takes no extra time to be mindful
If you are washing the dishes aware or unaware
the time factor is the same
The difference is by being unaware you are asleep
going nowhere
By being aware you are awake
being everywhere

The past is a memory within a dream
The future is the becoming within a dream
The Now is a fleeting moment
Once here
it is gone faster than the speed of light
So where is life living?

If not in the past or the future
and the Now slips through your fingers
Where is experience experienced?

Experience is unexplainable to scientists
The mystics write about it in poetry
The musicians play music to express it
The artists splash colors of paint to see it
But where is it?

The closest explanation of experience is by observing an infant
The infant senses what feels good or not
If it feels good
she smiles
If it does not feel good
she cries
No thinking and timeless

Experience is beyond time and space
It is the mingling of the inner and outer sensations
of consciousness
With no interference from thoughts
Once the infant is given a name
time and space are introduced
Experience then becomes a condition

A condition of conceptual thoughts from the beliefs passed down
from family and societal agreements
embedded from mass consciousness
Experience now becomes a *labeled symbol*
A labeled symbol of what you think it is not what actually is
This is called indirect perception
A perception filtering through the thoughts
of conditions and symbols
You feel the symbol hot
You see the symbol sky
You love the symbol mother
This condition is taken as real and unchanging
You are taken as real and unchanging
This is the dream
When sleeping and having a dream
it seems so real until you wake up
When living your life
it seems so real until you wake up
Waking up is called Direction Perception
A Perception of direct and intimate encounters with
Absolute Self
Beyond symbols and conditioning
If life is a dream
how do you live it?
By being 100% attached and 100% non-attached
and living within the Gap of the precise balance
where the two meet
It is called living in the Present
Living in the Present is
where the spark of experience ignites

THE SHOOTING STAR

A child and her grandmother went outside to admire the night sky. They both sat down on lawn chairs and viewed the endless universe. The child was quiet for a moment and then asked the grandmother, "Where do the stars come from?"

The grandmother replied, "They come from the space of creation."

The child continued to look up and said, "Where does the moon come from?"

Again the grandmother stated, "From the space of creation."

"Where does the darkness and light come from?"

The same answer was repeated by the grandmother, "The space of creation."

The child, with a quizzical look on her face and feeling a bit confused said, "Where is this space of creation?"

"It is within you." The grandmother said with a knowing look.

"You mean I created the stars, moon, and universe? I don't remember doing that."

"If you were not here admiring the stars, would they be here?" the grandmother asked. "You allow the existence of the stars to exist and to be enjoyed."

The child continued, "If I was not here, maybe someone else would be looking at them."

"True," the grandmother replied. "And that someone else is also allowing their existence to exist. The space of creation is you and all the other yous who occupy this Earth. It could only be within you."

The grandmother paused with a contemplative look on her face. "When you look at the stars, when you see the moon, where are you seeing them?" asked the grandmother.

"In the sky," the child answered.

"Where are you seeing the sky?" the grandmother asked.

"In my eyes."

"Where are your eyes seeing?"

"In my brain," the child reasoned.

The grandmother had an intense look in her eyes. "And where is your brain seeing it?" she asked abruptly.

"In me!" the child shouted. The child took a moment to reflect on her answer.

The silence grew and a glaze grew over the grandmother's eyes, and she spoke quietly—very quietly:

The eyes are the windows that allow you to look out
from within
The space of creation is where all is connected
This is where the Oneness is met
and where the constructs of beliefs and thoughts reside
Beliefs and thoughts make up your perception of the world
and enable you to experience the world as you see it within
There is no world outside of you
The stars can only be here if you are here

Do you see how important you are?

Suddenly a shooting star raced across the sky. They both gasped in wonder and became very still. The child broke the silence. "Yes, I am important," the child stated confidently. "But Grandma, if the brain sees the stars within me, where is *me*?

The grandmother took a long and deep breath and with a great big smile said, "That will be for another day."

They both laughed so hard tears rolled down their faces. The child jumped up and hugged her grandmother and whispered in her ear, "Thank you."

⌇

I am not saying that thoughts are bad
Thoughts play a very important role in your physical expression
They navigate through your physicality
and are necessary in the creation of your world

What I am saying is how careless you are with these
incredible powerhouses
Thoughts are not you
They are instruments of your free will to create what you wish
Enabling the enjoyment of the physical world
through your senses
You are the Thinker of thoughts

When you give power to thoughts and allow them to live
without direction and guidance
you are at the will of insanity
Resembling out-of-control horses

Please note:
The power of the horse is at your command
A respectful relationship and honoring its strength is required
You hold the reins

The power of thought is also at your command
A respectful relationship and honoring its strength is required
You hold the focus

When you direct your thoughts with Eternal Source
It has no other recourse but to manifest

Life is observed as being separate
as though it is not a part of you
It is you
All aspects of you and You
Thoughts come before matter
Thoughts come before matter

Thoughts are the connecting force that begin
the forming of your reality

The steps are as follows:
A reoccurring thought forms belief
A reoccurring belief becomes embodied feelings
The embodiment of *belief-feelings* vibrate
The vibration summons the atoms to obey that frequency
The frequency summons experience
Thus
you are experiencing your beliefs called reality

The ancients knew this

If you are not conscious of your Consciousness
If you do not know the cycle of creation
you are creating haphazardly

An eye cannot see that it sees
An ear cannot hear that it hears and so on
with all the other senses
They only know of themselves upon reflection

Color is perceived through the reflection of color
then the eye becomes aware of itself
A song is heard through the reflection of sound
then the ear becomes aware of itself
and so on with all the other senses
If it was not for the reflection of color or song
the eye and ear would not be known

The same principles apply to the personal self
It is only known upon reflection
The senses and personal self are deeply connected
Both sharing a focus of an outward motion
Yet
all of experience is within the inner motion
This is the mystery of *maya*
The illusion of life
The dream

If your perception is limited through the personal self only
you will remain within the dream
and never wake up
Remember
the personal self or ego cannot see itself
It is only known upon the awareness of the reflection
in your Life's Picture
Wake up!
And be conscious of your Consciousness
This will lead to the Divine Perception
and reveal the cycle of creation is sitting in your seat

Trying to control aspects of your life that are not controllable
is a disconnect from the stream of well-being
And an expression of not feeling safe
There is no such thing as control
Can you control a river?

There is a path of least resistance
or in other words
a path of cooperation

Moving with the flow and surrendering to Current
allows you to exercise your power of direction
Not the misplaced power of trying to control the Current
Your ego is not the source of Current
It is not the Supreme Authority
It thinks it is
but it is not
When you try to control the uncontrollable
it is a dam holding back the rushing waters of the Universe
However
the dam cannot hold it back for too long
It will burst
To move with the eternal Current
Alignment is required through focused thoughts
and the feelings of love and joy
Let go
Let be

Then the forces of the Universe
will be in collaboration with you
creating what is necessary for the Grand Balance
⸙

Pay attention
Beings share One Mind
It appears to be you and the other
However
it is One

The waters of the world
share One Liquid
It appears to be rivers and lakes
oceans and rain
However
it is One

One Mind contains all the thoughts ever thought
One Liquid contains all water ever shed

When you focus on a thought with feelings
the frequency of that thought intensifies
The thought is embraced by similar thoughts of the One Mind
creating momentum

It is much the same as a drop of rain falling into the river
The waters of the river embrace the raindrop and
push it along with the current's momentum

The contents of the mind of Hitler
are as accessible as the contents of the mind of Jesus or Gandhi

It all depends on the focus of thought
and the feelings feeding it

CߠP

Letting go
is the laying down within the palms of the Universe
and not to take on a burden that is not yours

Look all around
The intricate doings of nature and humanity

The flower does not think about blooming
It just blooms
The clouds do not think about moving with the wind
They just move
The birds do not think about singing their songs
They just sing
The body does not think about breathing
It just breathes

The same applies to the Earth orbiting the sun
and the moon orbiting the Earth
They just orbit

The same applies to you

There is a divine intelligence
that is directing every particle of matter
in a symphony called Life

To think that we are bigger than *That*
is totally crazy

SACRED MOMENT ON EXPANSION

Expansion and growth are the natural aspects of evolution. If nothing expanded or grew, life would not be living. As a matter of fact, it would not exist. The seed expands into a grand tree. The egg expands into a chicken. The caterpillar expands into a butterfly. The infant expands into an adult. The universe is a symbol of the expansiveness within us all. We are meant to thrive.

Expansion with no interference or resistance will eventually become One from which it originated, your Home. The yogis have a term explaining this cycle, *Tat Tvam Asi—I AM That.*

MEDITATION

Gently close your eyes; inhale and exhale for three cycles. Focus on the rising and falling of your breath. Now ask yourself, *Where is my home?* Inhale and exhale slowly for another three cycles.

Breathe normally continuing to focus on the breath. Fine-tune your focus on *That* from which the inhale originates and *That* which the exhale falls back into. *That* is where you reside, your Home. You come from *That*; you return to *That*. The breath is a constant reminder.

Continue the focus on your breath for three to five breath cycles. Slowly open your eyes and move through your day or night, knowing your Home is always with you.

Awake
You are not of this world
⌒⥀⌒

15

IF THE POT IS TOO HOT ...
GET OUT

Pain is the indicator signaling what you really want

If it hurts
get out
If it is painful
get out
If it is fearful
get out
If the pot is too hot
get the hell out

Turn the heat down by not staying in the same
round-robin of thought and belief
Recognize the boil
of guilt and regret
unworthiness and fear
shame and anger
It has been bubbling for a very long time
with no real purpose

When the mist clears and all the water has evaporated
the heat of the pot is too much to endure
And the scars begin to develop
Do not wait too long

Use the pot to cook something delicious
You are the chef
The master of the kitchen
Put in the ingredients you like
Gently stir and smell the aroma
Yum
And taste the wondrous cuisine of your creation

There is a stream of well-being intertwined within existence
It is the fabric of life's design

This stream consists of joy and forwardness
expansiveness and acceptance
compassion and love
Always in the direction of balance
Never unwavering
It is literally the constitution of the act of Becoming

Becoming is always becoming more of what it is
never less than what it was

All is well
even if it appears to be not well

The cycle of birth and death is necessary for the Divine Balance
Creating the space for growth and change
Allowing the expression of Eternal Source

Life would not live without growth and change

Eternal Source is the changeless stream of well-being
pushing through change to be recognized

Mistakes you have made in the past
that are still affecting you in the present
are blocking your happiness

Holding on
by not forgiving yourself
Beating yourself up with
guilt and fear
regret and shame

Mistakes
are opportunities to *take two*

You are the director of your life's story

You might have missed the first take

Take two
and do it differently
Even if it requires three or four takes

If you are still allowing past mistakes to haunt you
the only mistake you are actually making is bringing them into
the Now

⌒⊸⌒

SACRED CONVERSATION

Question: I feel confused and lost at times. How do I get a
clearer vision of the meaning of my life?

Answer: *Be still and connect with your True Self*
the highest perspective of you

Question: How does that help?

Answer: *This is the vision where you are standing*
on the highest summit
overlooking the valley of your life

The beauty is overwhelming
The pieces that appeared to be missing
are in their place

The whole is complete and you are found

THE WAY

Once upon a time there was a very unhappy man. He had great dreams of being a traveler, author, and inventor. He wanted peace, love, and joy in his life. However, his wife was in the way. His wife would not let him do or be what he desired. So he thought. So he believed.

His wife was very demanding and controlling. She was very fearful of anything new. She always tried to stop her husband from what he wanted to do by asking these questions:

"What if you get hurt?"

"What about money?"

"What would happen to me?"

The husband was a dedicated man, a responsible man who felt he had to sacrifice his life for her. He went to his hated job every day, cleaned the house, and took care of his wife. And at nine o'clock every evening he went to bed.

He never made any attempt to follow his dreams. He kept his dreams hidden in the dream state and dared not to bring them into the waking state. When he was dreaming, he felt most alive and awake. In his waking state, he was the walking dead: victimized, trapped, and hopeless.

Eventually, his wife died. He missed her. They did have some good times together and she was always filling the house with talk and aromas from her cooking. Now, he felt empty and lost.

A few months later, he was having a drink with a friend at a local pub. The friend was going on a trip and asked him to come along with him.

"Oh no, I cannot go," said the man.

"Why?" asked the friend.

"Oh my, what could happen if I leave?" continued the man.

"What if I get hurt?"

"What about money?"

"What will happen to me?"

The man stood up and cried in panic, "I am not allowed!"

"Not allowed by whom?" asked his confused friend.

The man thought for a moment and stated quietly under his breath, "By me." An insight flashed throughout his being:

My wife was not in the way
I was in the way because of my fears
and I used her as an excuse and to blame
She was not in the way
She was the Way
The Way to face my fears and honor my desires
I Am the Way
or I am in the Way
Which do I choose now?

Filled with joy and revelation, he turned to his friend and shouted, "I am going with you! I finally realized the reason why I did not follow my dreams."

"Great," said the friend with a big smile on his face.

"I just wish I had known this sooner," continued the man. " I missed so much time."

"There is only now, my friend; now is the perfect time." His friend smiled. "Let's go!" And they both briskly walked to the travel agent.

New desires require new beliefs
The path is tight at times

Focus is the key

Pinpoint your mind on one thing
The one thing becomes everything

Floating in nothingness and everythingness
Yet
rooted in Presence

Squeeze through the pinpoint

Until you decide to let go
it may be uncomfortable

There is no turning back
Back does not exist

Pop through the other side
Take deep breaths
And admire the new landscape

Stay as long as you feel joy

For there is another pinpoint waiting for you

When you are afraid to give
you are in fear of being taken
When you are afraid to love
you are in fear of accepting your worthiness

When you are afraid of pleasure
you are in fear of losing control
When you are afraid of expressing your feelings
you are in fear of feeling your feelings

Here is a reassurance

When you give from Heart
there is nothing to be taken
When you love from Heart
you know your birthright of Magnificence

When you enjoy pleasure from Heart
there is nothing to control
When you express from Heart
your Feelings are not yours

The body expresses through feelings
The mind expresses through thoughts
Eternal Source expresses through Heart

Move from the heat of pain
which you have been fanning with fear and protection
to the warmth of love and trust
that only Heart knows

⌒

When the outside world has the same repeated results
that are not pleasing to you
What are your avenues of thoughts?

Thoughts are the avenues of energy
allowing similar frequencies of circumstance to connect
with you
Your thoughts are avenues stating
Come this way

Like attracts like
Even when it is not liked

If an unpleasing event or encounter
is in your circumstance repeatedly
watch your thoughts
Change your focus from the alluring attraction
and addiction of thought
to being the observer of thought

The avenues will be interrupted

The only reality of thought is your choice of thinking it

Remember
Life's Picture is the familiar movie
It is within the matrix of your Being
The energy blueprint from thought
Circuiting over and over again

You are watching the same movie over and over again
Maybe different characters
Maybe different names and places
Nevertheless
the same movie is playing

You are in front of your ticket booth every moment
Is it time to buy a different ticket?

⌒⊚⌒

Walking down the street
I AM standing right in front of you
I AM trying to get your attention always

The brief meeting of the eyes of a passerby
A bird's song in the midst of traffic noise
A missed step of your walk
A small flower growing on the side of the road

However
you are too busy looking down
Too busy with noisy thoughts
Too busy trying to figure out solutions from a solutionless place

You cannot solve a problem from the same thinking
that created the problem

Look up!

Here *I AM*

The heart is the portal to the eternal
108 Nadis
Energy channels of the body
Joining at the heart center
to sing the beat of consciousness and love

The physical heart is the receiver for Heart
Heart is Eternal Love
Speaking the universal language for all of Earth's kingdoms
Mineral and plant
animal and human
When open to Heart
the highway to God is open
Connecting to *All That Is*
Answering all the questions and presenting all the solutions
to all of the problems
Heart is what fuses
It is the whole greater than the sum of its parts
The center of the Being's community
Integrating not separating
Separation closes the portal
Blind to the Sight we all yearn to know
Integration opens the portal
Seeing who you are is
what everything else Is

Recognition of this is nothing new
It has always been and always will be
Sight is Seen by closing your eyes
and opening your Heart

THE DRUG EFFECT

I was watching one of the many, many commercials about drug medications on the television. There seems to be so many people experiencing physical complications and pain nowadays. The drugs appear to be a magical substance to bring happiness and relief from pain and discomfort.

In the commercial, everyone was smiling and living full and happy lives. Scenes of people jogging, picnicking with friends and family, painting, dancing, and sitting by the ocean were often flashed on the screen.

Meanwhile in the background the announcer was warning of the side effects:

"You may experience headaches, depression, stomach ulcers, difficulty breathing, blurred vision, possible blindness, suicidal thoughts, bleeding, vomiting, loss of balance, heart attacks, stroke, blood clots, and there have been reported cases of people developing cancer and life-threatening infections. If you have any of these side effects, contact your doctor immediately."

After a moment of pondering, a Voice came to me:

Connect with your Eternal Source or God
Take a dose of love and compassion for yourself and others
daily
Listen to the intelligence of your body
Observe your avenues of thoughts and beliefs
Assume responsibility for your life and what you create
However
you may experience serious side effects such as:
feeling light and energetic
creative and giving
loving and joy

And there have been reported cases of bliss
and serious enlightening moments
If you are having any of these effects
please contact your Greater Self immediately
and say thank you

After saying thank you and having a good laugh, I turned off the television and walked away.

⤴

The voices in my head
Are they me?
Voices of
judgment and guilt
shame and control
negativity and fear
They are speaking 70,000 times a day

Why would I put myself through this?
Who is talking?
They seem to have a life of their own
At times the voices certainly do not feel good
They all live in the past of depression and regret
or the future of anxiety and worry
What is the point?
Enough!

If I am noticing and being aware of the voices
the voices cannot be who I am
Who *I Am* is the one noticing

These voices are programmed thoughts of belief
Creating the flesh of the body
The body feels it and the mind thinks it
over and over again
Molding the physicality of experience
Take control

I AM directs the voices
not the voices directing who *I AM*

Life is a swirl of *All Is Well*
Penetrating every aspect of existence
Emanating a steady stream of love

When the outside world appears to be going crazy
All Is Well may be difficult to find
Fear sets in and separateness surfaces
Along with sadness and feelings of doom
We try to fix the world by laws and restrictions
By locking doors and erecting walls
By wars and sophisticated weapons
Focus is on the outer
As though the remedy is in the world
If you cut a weed
it may appear to be gone for a short time
Let me assure you it will grow back two-and three-fold
The weed's growth is not in the weed
It is in the root and the preparation of the soil
When we lock the doors
to keep out
the opposite occurs
it is kept in
Crazy occurs
when crazy is within mass and individual consciousness
As well as within you
It takes a brave soul to accept this
and impeccable courage to change it
Hear the human cries for love
And the primal screams to merge with Eternal Source
Stay in the swirl or bolt the door
And look for the evidence in the world of your choice

Three very simple insights to live by:

Focus is the key
Love of Self is the way
Joy is the purpose

That's it!

⟡

SACRED MOMENT ON
BEING UNCOMFORTABLE

When in the hot seat and feeling uncomfortable, move! Move from the uncomfortable heat of pain. If you are sitting on a nail, do you continue to sit on it or do you move? Feeling uncomfortable is the signal not to stay put. It is the acknowledgement of what you do not want any longer, and it is time to focus on what you do want.

If you are in chaos, know you want peace.
If your body is in pain, know you want relief.
If you are in fear, know you want the safety of love.

Being uncomfortable is the sacred sign of the desire to be comfortable within the movement of expansion. You need to turn your sight inward. This is where your big, soft, comfortable chair is waiting for you.

MEDITATION

Gently close your eyes; inhale and exhale slowly for three cycles. Imagine being on a soft raft floating on the ocean, feeling totally safe. Your body is relaxed, light, and supported by the raft as it rocks gently with the waves. The sun is warming your body perfectly. You slide your hand into the cool water. As you open your mind's eye, you see the bluest sky with one puffy white cloud drifting by. Close your mind's eye and let go … just let go.

Enjoy this state for a few moments. When you are ready, count slowly from the numbers five to one, being more relaxed with each declining number. When you reach the number one, slowly open your eyes and keep peace with you always.

⌒⌒⌒

16

∞

BE RESPONSIBLE! HAVE FUN

Intimacy of life lies within having fun

Play is the dance of life
Play is the opportunity to be intimate
This is when you are having fun
and more importantly
fun has you

Fun is fun
There is no denying
Some look upon play as childish
Irresponsible
Not for the mature
Rubbish!

Responsibility is not performing a duty
Responsibility is responding to yourself
and doing what you enjoy

Consciousness and play are one package
Fun is playing with the magick and wonder of life
It is laughter
It is enjoyment
Lightheartedness
It is living consciously
Play is not for the young only
It comes with the territory of
Growth and Balance

Be responsible!
Play and have fun
Then life's workings will no longer be a secret
⤜⤏

Games are amusing and fun
The excited anticipation of the outcome is the joy of it all
Win or lose

The game of life is in motion
Life's melodrama of
happiness and sadness
frustration and accomplishment
are all part of the game
The excited anticipation of the outcome is the joy of it all
Ups or downs
The ups are experiencing height
and the downs are the push for higher ground
Acknowledge this

Become a master game player
The queen of the game is the most versatile and valued
The pawn of the game is the most limited and least valued
Are you royalty over your kingdom or a pawn for others to use?
By knowing the game of human existence
you are making the decisions where your pieces move
You will always win

Not knowing the game
you allow others to make the decisions
where your pieces move
You will always lose
Remember
Games are played to have fun
Life is lived to have fun

SACRED CONVERSATION

Question: What is fun?
Answer: *Fun is focused in the Now*
                 No thoughts of the past or future
                 Enjoyment in the purest form
                 Totally absorbed in the doing
                 It is laughter and freedom
                 wrapped up in the energy of joy
                 And the melding of you and You

Question: How do I have fun?
Answer: *Watch the children*
                 The masters of fun
                 Totally mindful in a
                 seemingly mindless activity
                 Dance in the wind
                 Sing your heart out and
                 laugh until your belly aches
                 Hold hands with the Divine
                 and skip into the sunset

The hills and valleys of life
Up and down
Down and up
Depths of despair and heights of bliss

Nausea can erupt
With this roller coaster ride
Some call the Cyclone
Especially when holding on to the ups and resisting the downs
Making it more difficult to go with the flow

The roller coaster is a ride
A ride only
Go with the fun
Put your hands up and scream
Yippee!

It could be scary at times
But know when it is down
it will head right back up again

No matter how terrifying the ride
after it is done
you are ready to go for another ride

IN EVERY SPECK

Once upon a time, there was a young woman who had a strong desire to be enlightened. She meditated five times a day for long periods of time, sitting on hard surfaces. She fasted and practiced extreme austerity. She donated her time to the shelters, orphanages, and hospitals and never had time for personal enjoyment. The woman felt that she needed to feel pain to feel the love of God. Every day she would say, "Please, God, I want to be enlightened. I want to know you."

When she serviced the people and performed her spiritual practice, *sadhana,* her face always looked sad and intense, which eventually formed deep wrinkles on her forehead and a longing in her eyes ... always waiting.

She never bought anything for herself. She wore sandals in the winter and owned one article of clothing. "I want to see God!" she cried. Every night, she fell asleep with her face drenched in tears. She sacrificed all personal desires and gave up all possessions, living a life alone and poor. She grew old and unfulfilled.

One day, she was sitting in the park, watching the children play. One child came up and said, "Are you a sage?"

"I am a woman of God," she replied.

The child looked at her with a confused look on his face and said, "Then why do you look so sad? We play with God every day, and we are always laughing. As a matter of fact, God loves to play basketball, and I think she cheats."

The woman started to laugh uncontrollably and could not stop. She could not catch her breath, and her eyes filled with tears—tears of joy this time, not sadness or extreme yearning.

A light flashed through her body, and she saw God in the little boy and in everything around her.

A butterfly landed on her nose, she gazed into the insects eyes, and she became lost in the moment. Time stopped.

As she wiped her tears of joy, she heard a Voice:

Laugh and have fun
Lighten up
I AM in every speck of existence
laughing with you over the absurdity of life

What is your first responsibility?
It is not your job
It is not paying your bills
It is not even your family

Your first responsibly is being in happiness
by being in Partnership with your True Self
A force greater than you that conducts the order of life

Just observe
The trees reaching for the sun
The feel of the wind brushing across your face
The breath's motion
The light in a child's eye
The beat of your heart

All in concert with You
All you have to do is be with You
Fostered by feelings of gratitude
compassion and love

Being happy first is not selfish
It is the ultimate form of selflessness

When you are aligned with your True Self
it joins forces with you
propelling your actions
How can this be selfish?
Selfishness does not exist within this state of consciousness

What benefit is there in being unhappy
worried and anxious?
Creating separation

At times
our human interactions can create
uncomfortable circumstances
When this occurs
it is a sign you momentarily lost your way from Partner
Once acknowledged
your only responsibility is to join forces again

Partner did not leave
you did

Assume your responsibility
You will never be alone in taking care of your family
job and bills

Partner holds your hand through all adversity and good fortune
You are an entity of One encompassing both
The supreme intimate relationship

A relationship unveiling the
Ultimate Responsibility of being a good Partner

⌁

Be conscious of the Awareness that is Conscious of you
The Cycle of Enlightenment
The Cycle allows your unconscious embodiment
called your body
to become mindful
Mindfulness enables the bypassing
of the circuitry of unconsciousness

We collect data in our lifetimes and believe it to be true
It is stored as flesh
It is called embodiment

The body allows the interaction of
the data between the inner and outer worlds
It is called experience

Thoughts interpret experience
It is stored as beliefs
It is called perception

Perception is the Field of the world's fiber
Fleeting yet enduring

Where are you?
In the flesh?
In the thought?
In the perception?
Yes
you are *in all*
Yet
not *of all*

Awareness of the pulse of unconsciousness and consciousness
of mortality and immortality
specific location and omnipresent
is the *Cycle of Enlightenment*
Where are You?

Simultaneously
you are playing in the Field and Witnessing the play as well

We are taught for every cause there is an effect
It certainly appears that way
We are taught the shortest distance
from here to there is a straight line
It certainly appears that way
We are taught a tree is real
It certainly appears that way

We are also taught happiness is in the world
Look under every stone and tell me where is it?
I think we have it backwards

The cause of every effect was affected as well
Cause and effect are one

There and here are not separate locations
Once you are there
you are here
There and here are one

The tree is not outside of you
It is seen and interpreted within
The tree and you are one

This is a difficult concept to grasp
However
the hold is loosening through the merging
of Spirituality and Science
Step aside from your limited sight of duality
and allow the true Vision to come forth

We are taught that God is outside of you
It certainly appears that way

To know the existence of God
God has to exist in you
God and you are One

Watching the movement of the river
Never a moment standing still
Never a moment remaining the same
A thought surfaced how the river relates to life

Everything in life is temporary and impermanent
Nothing remains the same
But we act as though everything will last forever
That's pretty funny

The young have tons of energy and very little wisdom
The aged have tons of wisdom and very little energy
That's pretty funny

Nothing is real
All is an illusion within a living dream of one's perception
believing a reality of unshakable facts and truths
That's pretty funny

We work a lifetime to accumulate money
and it cannot be taken with us when the body dies
That's pretty funny

In this life we are young with strong bodies and tight skin
and it turns into weak bodies with loose skin
That's pretty funny

Life is just a fleeting moment
no past and no future
That's really funny

We live as though this body is our true identity
Our true identity is not this body
That's pretty serious

Focus is on the temporary
and mortality is treated as immortality
That's pretty serious

We have the opportunity
to feel the love and essence of *All That Is*
That's pretty serious

Creation is in our hands
Life's journey can be filled with purpose and empowerment
Being a victor not a victim
That's really serious

We thirst for enlightenment
Religions and spiritual groups are very serious
about their ideas and practices
That's pretty funny ... because
enlightenment is knowing the joke:

Life is very serious in a funny sort of way

When you dream
the dream is not in your head only

The dream is an *expansive energy*
that extends out beyond your body
connecting with similar forces for it to become alive
Stay in the focus of dream
and allow it to dream of its becoming
It will form and give signals to you
on where and how to move into action

Knowing the power of dreaming
is knowing the essence of creation
If the power is not recognized
it will stay in the hidden
And extreme discomfort will develop

Your dream is waiting for you
Do the necessary preparations
The preparation of believing in it
The preparation of listening to its instructions and directions
The preparation of becoming it
The instructions are not written or spoken
They are communicated through
synchronicity and desire
nudging and insight
excitement and joy

Dreams expand the world
Walk into your dream
and allow it to become alive

An animal does not say thank you or please
for the caretaking you offer
It is love's service

It is expected

They know their Godliness
Therefore
giving the opportunity for you to know yours

Giving empties
Leaving a space for allowing

Allowing Godliness
to know ItSelf

Fun is in the beat of your heart
The heart beats to the tones and music of your existence

When you are excited
the beat speeds up to the dance of bliss
When you are at peace
it beats to a calm rhythm of contentment
When you are inspired
the beat is in alignment with Spirit and can hardly be heard
When you are in love
there are more spaces between the beats to receive

When the music becomes out of tune because of stress and fear
it has no rhythm and the music is not pleasing
This is not good for the heart
This is not good for you

The heart always looks for fun and joy
the true connectors
It is the center of that energy
It is the receptor of existence

Everything wants to have fun
A tree is chopped down
The branches start to grow immediately
and reach for the sun to dance in the breeze once again

The river is blocked by rocks and boulders
The water will start immediately to find another way
around and over them to continue
the graceful movement of flow

Listen to your Heart
The beat is universal
The message
however
is only for you to understand

༄

Do we have any original or new thoughts?
The Answer:
The only originality is what you do with the
expression of the thought's stream of energy
Remember
All That Is
is already

Every body of water
is all the water
already
It is not new water
It is recycled over and over again
Every thought that is thought
is in the Field of Mind
already
There are no new thoughts
They are recycled over and over again
However
when thought is received
your expression of it is a slightly different version
Creating a slightly different version of thought
to be recycled again
Let it be known
In the Field there is no time
no past or future
And within the present holds All
Every thought ever thought is in the Field of Mind
Send your Invitation
and be aware of who and what you are inviting

Constant motion of *still frames* is the movie of life

Each frame is the image of the thought strongly believed
Crystallized by feelings
The shot is taken
Projected in a set sequence we call *experiencing reality*

The movie editor takes the sequences of the frames
and connects them with an idea
When projected on the screen
it appears to be one continuous movement

Physicality is experienced the same

Life sequences are the *still images* of thought
and are connected by the incredible light speed of belief

Life is a movie that is being played over and over again
with the sequences of thought from
mass consciousness and your individual experiences

To see a different life movie
the whole sequence does not have to change

All that has to change is one frame of thought

SACRED MOMENT ON
FUN

Fun is an art: the balance of enjoyment and earthly needs. Fun feeds the Soul; it creates not destroys. It does not take from or cause an expense for others. Fun is timeless and brings you into the moment. It ranges from the silly realm to the realm of your passions.

When having fun, take a moment to look all around you. You will hear the daisies cheering, see the trees dancing in the wind, and all of existence in concert with you. Fun is a necessary component for enlightenment and the evolution of consciousness. Fun is the fuel for expansion. It allows the comparison of contrast to bring awareness to your desires. Fun is individual preference; however, it is universally preferred.

As we get older, we forget what it is to have fun and become much too serious. A crust begins to form around Heart and Soul. Break though; become flexible. Do not dismiss fun. Be responsible ... have fun.

MEDITATION

Gently close your eyes; inhale and exhale slowly for three cycles. Remember a time when you had fun, when your whole being was in the activity—no thoughts or worries. It could be a time when you were young and playing with friends or a time when you were laughing so hard, tears rolled down your face and you could not catch your breath, or maybe a time when you were totally absorbed in the creative process or playing with your children and animals.

Play it over in your mind for a minute or two: feel the feelings, see the surroundings, and hear the sounds. In your mind's eye, walk to a mirror or a still pond and look at your face: smiling, clear eyes, and a bright face. Stay with this image for a few moments.

Inhale and exhale slowly. As you open your eyes gently, bring that image and, most importantly—the feelings of that image—into the day. Have fun!

17

TINY-ITTY-BITTY SPACE

Within the Gap of transition
the potential of the ordinary can become the extraordinary

The *Gap*
A Tiny-Itty-Bitty Space

Between all things
all thoughts
all actions
Between the sunrise and sunset
Between the breath and lifetimes

This Tiny-Itty-Bitty Space
is where the world is created
It holds the immensity of every dream that *was* and *will* be
A dimension with no dimension
yet
all dimensions are included

Great minds used this Tiny-Itty-Bitty Space
Newton and Edison
Beethoven and Curie
just to name a few
Upon entering the ordinary
the extraordinary happens
It is where the spectacular is born

It is between the sleep and wake states
Not totally awake
yet
not totally asleep

Many artist and mystics
philosophers and scientists
writers and inventors
use this Tiny-Itty-Bitty Space
to break through thick walls of ignorance

When the walls are down
a quick glimpse of this Tiny-Itty-Bitty Space
reveals that it is not so tiny

The *Gap* is vast and boundless
immeasurable and omnipresent
Touching from the quark of an atom
to the galaxies of the universe
and beyond

Holding every possible possibility

Joy lives within magick of simplicity
The sun's imprint upon the trees
Sweet sounds of silence
Comfort of a soft chair

When joy is felt
the body forgets any discomfort
and *all is well* lives

The art of magick
uses the natural forces to uncover the beauty of the mundane
The magick is within every breath
Don't let the thoughts of discomfort interfere with joy

Discomfort has a momentum
It is a habit reoccurring
The neurological groove has grown deep

Magick is at our fingertips
Belief allows it to be touched

The trick is
open the door to the belief and wonder of magick
then the magick of belief will be in motion

At times
we are dangling on the *rope of beliefs* that do not serve us
Causing pain and confusion

The *rope of beliefs* is an energetic network
that connects and ties the inner and outer worlds together
If you were standing in the world of the mystics
the rope would look like a luminous funnel
Moving and swaying like a snake
Searching for belief connections between you and the world
Tying the knot and claiming it to be true
By holding on to the rope
you may never find what is right under your feet
or what is above your head

The depths of belief are revealed through scaling up the rope
and finding its connections to the world
The depths of surrender are revealed by letting go of the rope
and realizing the connections to the world are insignificant

To scale up or release the rope
leads to the same realization
However
climbing the rope is exhausting
releasing the rope is a relief

Don't just hold on
Make up your mind
climb the rope or let go

⸻

Where the sky meets the ocean
knowledge is achieved

No matter how hard you try
the horizon could never be reached
Distance determines the sight
The farther you are the more real it appears
The closer you are the illusion becomes evident
To reach it is impossible

What is the knowledge that lies between the sky and ocean?

It is the knowledge
without facts
without proofs
It is a knowledge that is a direct experience
without any static from thoughts

In the world of duality
if there is an up
a down must exist
if there is happiness
sadness must exist

Duality is the proof of the other
Actually there is no other
Therefore
neither exist
Upon closer examination
duality is born from the mindscape of One

The horizon is seen by the eye
Confirmed through conversation
Artists paint it
Poets write about it
Yet
to find it
never will it be
Life and the horizon share the same landscape

The Knowledge lies in knowing this
and how it applies to all of life's process in this physicality

The horizon exists to be able to enjoy experience

Embrace it
admire it
and smile at this wondrous illusion called Life

Way way way back
if an apple was wanted
one had to grow an apple tree from a seed and wait for fruition
Way way back
someone thought of growing apple trees
And if an apple was wanted
one could go in the orchard and pick it
Way back
someone thought of growing apple trees and
selling the apples
And if an apple was wanted
one could go to the market during the season to buy an apple
Yesterday if an apple was wanted
one could go to the supermarket anytime of the year
to buy an apple

Today we are now approaching the time when
all we have to do is think of an apple
and one will have an apple
Maybe friends will knock on the door
and have an apple in their hands
Maybe an apple will be on the kitchen counter

The speed of retrieving information
from the internet is a reflection
of the speed and information available from our consciousness
Including the manifesting process of what is becoming

However
the internet still does not compare to what is at our command

The wait time is shrinking
The responsibility is expanding

What does this all mean?

We are ready to receive the Sacred Knowledge:
The world's creation is in our hands

⸎

As a human
you will always have many voices in your mind
However
the voices do not have to have you
Know the mechanism

Thought energy is the extended *energy form*
of your body's matrix
This holds the blueprint or configuration of you

The matrix is the environment of you *before it manifests as* you

When thought becomes belief
the matrix sets up the circuitry of those beliefs
Beliefs are then expressed through the body and feelings

The body is a composite and receptacle of these *energy forms*
There is constant exchange of vibration
vortexing in and out of the body
The same is true with how the magnetic field
of the Earth operates

A thought is thought
then believed
The *believed thought* in *energy form* hovers around the body
Inviting compatible thoughts of the world
Making the belief of that *energy form* stronger
The body sucks it back in and expels it back out to be sensed

Once sensed
the belief is believed to be real and the mind will look for
additional proof of its reality

This is the mechanism

The body is a compressed vibration of your beliefs
that attracts other *belief voices*
Hence
all the voices in your mind
Listen to the one Voice
which bypasses all the chatter of the other voices

The voiceless Voice of Love

SACRED CONVERSATION

Question: How can I accept miracles in my life?

Answer: *To accept miracles*
        you first have to accept Me
        the I AM of You

        Miracles cannot be born
        in the limited space of thinking
        Miracles need room to roam which I AM offers

        Know the distinction between
        thinking thoughts and receiving thoughts
        Thinking thoughts
        you are in the way
        Receiving thoughts
        you step aside

        Stay with Me always
        The unexpected will be expected every moment

Simple pleasures are often overlooked

The pleasures of
silence and enjoying a meal
a hot bath and warm bed
the fragrance of a flower

These simple pleasures give
peace and security
feelings of warmth and well-being

They are treasures more valuable
than a chest of gold and diamonds

Unfortunately
many pass these treasures in a frantic search for
peace and security
feelings of warmth and well-being

WONDERING ABOUT WHY

A student went up to her teacher and asked a million *whys* of the world. "We are extensions of God, are we not?" asked the student.

"Yes," replied the teacher.

The student rambled on with a number of questions:

> "Why do people hurt each other?"
> "Why can't we get along?"
> "Why are religions so hateful?"
> "Why do we harm our Mother Earth?"
> "Why is there so much fear?"
> "Why don't we trust and love each other?"
> "Why is there so much violence in the world?"
> "Why don't we give more?"
> "Why do we allow children to starve?"

The list went on for hours. "Please tell me why!" cried the student.

"Hmmm," said the teacher patiently and contemplatively. "I have a *why* too. *Why* are you asking?" The teacher held a penetrating gaze.

The student perked up and said, "If I can figure out the *whys*, then I will be able to understand the world and have the eternal answer to all the questions of life.

"Oh," said the teacher with a loving smile on her face. "*Why* is not the question to ask. *Why* comes from the mind. The mind is always in the state of logic, looking for a reason and place for everything to fit in a nice, neat package. Therefore, it fits in a place that already exists. No knowledge is attained. This is not where the answers are," said the teacher.

"So where are they?" said the student, with a confused look on her face.

The teacher looked up and became silent for a very long time. It seemed endless to the student. So much so that the student was feeling uncomfortable and squirmed a bit and forgot about the *whys* and just wanted the silence to end. Finally, the teacher spoke directly to her Heart:

It is not in the whys
It is in the wonder
Wonder about wonder

I wonder how a mighty oak tree comes
from a seed smaller than a penny
I wonder how the Earth moves and I do not feel it
I wonder where sky begins and ends
I wonder how my eyes see a star light years away
and could also see an ant just a few inches away
I wonder how this incredible body has lightning speed
communication between all the cells joining in community
and allowing me to Be

Wonder fosters admiration and wholeness
unexpected astonishment and miracles
As well as
knowledge of the inner realms and movement of change

This is what life is made of
Wonder is all around us and it is larger than logic and reason
It is the Dream itself

Everything is dreaming about what it is Becoming
From a seed of a weed to the cell of a fetus
The Becoming cannot fit into the small confines of whys

Why fosters commonality and separateness
expectedness and temporariness
As well as
ignorance and stagnation

The teacher again looked at the student and said, "The *whys* you are asking are good questions; however, they have no definite answers. For the answers will only change as humans change and evolve consciously with a vision of depth, not surface." She paused and smiled lovingly at the student and resumed talking:

Wonder will place you in the seat of the Observer
Allowing the insight to your questions
Without judgment or blame
Just love infused with Divine Knowledge
It is not in whys
It is within you
All is within you including what appears to be outside of you

The student bathed in the silence for a moment and said very quietly, "I *wonder why* I didn't know this?"

They laughed and hugged each other into the darkest of the night.

꩜

The desire to *becoming more*
is generated by *feeling less*

The impulse to action
is from being still

The wanting for change
is from being the same

The yearning for God
is from being human

The polarities stretching from Center
only to return once again back to Center
The Eternal Source from which it came

Nature is a good example
The seed in the darkness of Earth
stretches for the light of sun
and upon completion
returns to its origin
the Earth
All stretches from Center
All returns to Center

And everything in between is life

Where is your *Home*?
Is it your house?
Is it your town and state?
Is it your country and planet?
Where is it?
Your body may take up physical space
but where is your true residence?

Strange feelings are always lurking like a fish out of water
being uncomfortable in your dry surroundings
You are constantly searching for Home to satisfy the thirst
for the feelings of love and peace
joy and safety
and most importantly
belonging

No matter how much you distract or run away from yourself
Home is the quest
We search and search in this world and even lifetimes
It will never be found in the world
Between what is real and what is not real lives the answer

Look into another's eyes and see yourself looking back at you
If you walk into a room surrounded by mirrors
you may be surprised or even fearful
thinking people are in the room
When you notice the mirrors
you say
Oh! It's just me and no need to fret or fear

So where is your Home?
It is in between your thoughts
and the space of exchange between
the inhalation and exhalation
It is within silence and stillness

Be still and know God
Then you can walk through the door
Welcome Home

⌒

Bridges connect every aspect of life
In the world
Bridges connect land to land
cities to cities
buildings to buildings

In the body
Bridges connect
neurons to neurons
organs to organs
cells to cells
Most importantly
Heart to mind

Once Heart and mind are connected
with no static of interference
a bridge forms
A bridge allowing the mystical world
and the world of consciousness
to interact with the physical world and freely move to and fro

In the mystical world
Bridges connect
body and spirit
Earth and Heaven
outer and inner worlds

Imagination is key
It holds the images to be experienced in the physicality

Belief and recognition
become the bridge that allows
the *channel of conversing* between the worlds
When the image is lived in imagination
creation is ready for its birth

As you walk over the bridge
you may stop for a moment and look behind you
Laughing
Realizing there was really never a bridge
It was just a ploy to get you to move

There are dreams within dreams
All dreaming of becoming the dream
and exposing the secret

A realm of existence that is truly mysterious
Delve deep into the secret of the mystical
and Know without thoughts
The mystery of how a seed grows into a tomato
The mystery of birth and death
The mystery of the Earth floating in space

The mystical world is where the secret lies
It is holding up
what appears to be known
In the physical
standing in front of a tree
there is a you and a tree
In the mystical
there is neither a you nor a tree
This is the secret
The secret that all of creation is within you
No separation

Where does the world lie?
In you

Shh ... This secret is out
Living dreams are for those who Wake up
Dreams of living are for those who remain asleep

Magick is in every breath
Be still
Pay attention

Do not allow the past to define you
or the future to scare you

Like the breath
be free of both
Not holding on to the past or future
Not holding on to the inhalation or exhalation of breath

The magick is within the Now
Feeling the eternal beat of Heart
And witnessing the clouds rolling by
and flowers swaying gently in the wind
whispering Love

This is Liberation

❧

SACRED MOMENT ON
THE TINY-ITTY-BITTY SPACE

The magick of life lies in *Perception*: the viewpoint of the observer and the thinker of the thoughts. It is the dreamer experiencing the dream. When the personal mind and ego step aside, your True Self steps forward from silence and stillness ... *within the Tiny-Itty-Bitty Space*. The Tiny-Itty-Bitty Space is between your thoughts, breath, and actions. Know your residence within silence, stillness, and the Tiny-Itty-Bitty Space. It is connected to the Infinite, pointing to your Home.

MEDITATION

Gently close your eyes; inhale and exhale slowly. Focus your attention on the rising and falling of the breath. Continue breathing normally and slowly switch your focus to the *key points* of the cycle of the breath: the transition from the inhalation to the exhalation and again from the exhalation to the inhalation. The Tiny-Itty-Bitty Space is within the transition. It is the space that allows the inhalation to transition to the exhalation and the exhalation to transition to the inhalation. Focus on the transitions for three or more minutes.

The Tiny-Itty-Bitty Space between the cycle of breath is that doorway to the Infinite. Slowly open your eyes and continue your day knowing the mystical world of the Infinite is within every breath.

◦◦◦

18

THE SLEEPLESS SELF

Know the You that is observing you

Be aware of Awareness
conscious of Consciousness
for *It* is aware and conscious of you always

The part of you who *was*
is and always *will be*
The part of you that is in the space between your thoughts
The part of you that is in the transition of your
inhalation and exhalation
The part of you that seems to be slightly
behind and above your head
The part of you that joins you and Eternal Source

It is known by many names
Higher Self and Witness
Higher Consciousness and the Sleepless Self
True Self and the Observer
To know it
first recognize it:

You were a baby
Now an adult
Your body and feelings
thoughts and actions all changed
What remained the same?

You sleep
You awake
Having a good and sound sleep you recall the dream
If you were sleeping
who witnessed the dream?

Intellectually you know your body will perish
Family and friends will pass on by
Yet
you continue to have a sense of immortality
What is that part that death cannot touch?

Watch yourself
watch you
That which watches you dream as your body sleeps
That which remains the same through all the changes
That which has a clear view from the summit
That which is aware of you always
This is a glimpse of Higher Self
Your True Self

It is not higher than you
It is You
Your connection to *All That Is*
Your answers to all your questions
Your solutions to all your problems
Your guru

Within the present
knowing your past and holding your future dream
The dream of Becoming
Softly It speaks in feelings and insights
knowings and coincidences
synchronicities and realizations
However
loud is the impact

It does not give you warnings of what *not to do*
It gives you impulses of what *to do*

It is *That* which fills the room in dark silence
transmitting a strong Presence
It is *That* dose which allows the taste of Eternal Love

Know your Higher Self intimately with honesty and sincerity
No need to pretend
Then feel *It*
know *It*
speak with *It*
pray and meditate with *It*
Be It
Once you discover the foundation of who you are
You will know the foundation of what everything else Is

The body runs
Spirit watches
The body jumps
Spirit watches
The body sleeps
Spirit watches
The body awakens
Spirit watches

Watching and waiting
Like a patient old friend
waiting for you to recognize its Presence

Until you do
Spirit watches

Consciousness breeds gentleness and compassion

When the *Inner* turning turns
other than this cannot exist

You see with new lenses
the old are discarded

The movement of knowing the Beauty arises
along with a tear of the forgotten

To others
a raindrop falls on a leaf
To you
it is *That* touching *That*
arising to *This*

❦

Be in the presence of those who are home
A daisy and maple tree
A squirrel and stone
All different
At home and loving it
In their home you will be reminded of your Home
All of creation comes from you
Once realized
all returns back to you
Revealing the illusion of separation
This is meant by the term *Coming Home*

The Tao speaks of the returning motion
The yogis speak of self-realization
Jesus spoke of I and my father are one
The Native Americans speak of the Sacred Circle

Life's movement is circular
Similar to a wheel turning in the same place and the
center expanding eventually taking over the wheel

Once Home
you will realize you never left
Feelings of all the love you have yearned for
has always been with you
You will know where you live and it is not where your body lies

The *Internal Records* of your true family album will be located
This is the process of moving forward
to go Back from which you came

Creation starts from a sound
a vibration
a thought

A desire is also a sound
a vibration
a thought
This is what sparks the momentum of creation
The yogis say *Aum* is the primordial sound
The sound of sounds
If you listen
you will hear *Aum* in every
word and song
And even in the swirling of the wind

A sea of unlimited potentiality
Just waiting to be dipped into and bring forth
And what is it that dips into potentiality
and brings forth creation?
It is a vibration
a sound
a thought
a desire
Embodied within the symphony of feelings

The seeds of creation are seeds of thought
The seeds of thought are seeds of desire
The seeds of desire are seeds of intention
The seeds of intention are the intonations that sing your body

Similar to a farmer who plants the tomato seed in the soil
Giving the necessary conditions for growth
water and sun
love and attention
And stands by with excited anticipation for the fruit

The farmer did not actually produce the fruit
The farmer *set the conditions* for the fruit to grow

Your life is the same

You *set the conditions* for the seeds of desire to manifest
through the energy of belief and attitude
thought and love

Then step aside to allow the magick with Eternal Source
to do the work

Your work is to *set the conditions*
The work of *Eternal Source* is to produce

This is the reality of Reality

༺⚬༻

Divine Consciousness is the Totality of Magnificence
Mind is an expression of Divine Consciousness

Personal mind is the expression of you
that takes the credit and praise for the Totality of Magnificence
The ego directs this portion of the personal mind
It is the tip of the iceberg

Look inward to know its massive depths

The ego is a rock thinking it is a mountain
It is a drop of salt water thinking it is the ocean
And the personal mind supports this idea

The personal mind is conscious of its properties
But it is not the total Property

Mind is conscious including the personal mind
It is a dual-purposed window
It could look out into the world
and look back in

Once the ego is out of the equation
the drop of salt water remembers
and merges back into the ocean
the rock remembers
and becomes part of the mountain once again

The Totality of Magnificence is reinstated
And the personal mind knows its place

A thought came to mind
while in a solemn mood

Ah! you can't hold on to anything
money and people
they all pass by
The only thing you really have is yourself

Then a small Voice interrupts to clarify:

You *don't even have* yourself
You *see my child*
Self has you

The cells of the body
are a microcosm of the macrocosm
The cells reflect the process of human evolution
Humans are a
microcosm of the macrocosm
Humans reflect the process of Existence evolution

The cell's internal functions
are the same as a human's internal functions
Each cell operates individually with the whole body in mind
through lightning speed awareness and communication

The cell knows the whole picture and its work within the image
Its job is to keep the body alive
The cells know their *dharma*

Each cell's destiny is the same
Each human's destiny is the same
Coming from *That* which we go back *Into*

The cells would have no purpose to live
without the body
Humans would have no purpose to live
without Absolute Self

When a cell separates from the whole it is called
disease
creating havoc
When a human separates from the whole
it is called disunity
creating confusion

Many cells are dying every moment
New cells replace the dead cells immediately to maintain
balance
When a heart cell dies
a new heart cell slips into place
It fills the space that is needed and directed by the
Pull of Creative Intelligence

Many humans are dying every moment
Births replace the dead immediately to maintain balance
This is the way we choose to come into the physical
To fill the space that is needed and directed by the
Pull of Creative Intelligence

Once the whole picture is seen
you will know what to do within your space

The cell is an extension of the body
The human is an extension of Absolute Self

See yourself as a cell working individually
for the benefit of the whole scheme

You are not alone
You are a cell of the Cosmic Being

꩜

SACRED CONVERSATION

Question: It is inevitable that the body will perish.
               The yogis say we are immortal.
               Could this *be*?

Answer: You *hit the nail on the head*
               Just Be
               And the answer is yes

cↄ

Sometimes You and you
are not compatible

You wants to grow and be all you can be
Yet
you bring in resistance
fear and insecurity

You needs you
you needs You

Hold hands

When compatible
it is quite a ride of fun and excitement

All the possibilities are just behind the door
You open it
and sometimes you close it and even lock it

Take that first step
turn the door knob
It takes courage and trust to open the door

Be a good Partner
walk over the threshold

You will greet you
and take hold of your hand
as you skip down the road to yet another door

Communication has nothing to do with words
It has everything to do with impulses and feelings
The solar plexus is a divine guide
The third eye is Divinity's Sight

We have energy vortexes within the body
Along the spine
Each holds the frequencies of attraction
They are called *chakras*
Spinning to receive and give communication
from the inner and outer realms
Many years ago
yogis and other ancients spoke of these vortexes
There are seven associated with the body
as well as other chakras beneath and above the body

Each of the seven chakras have a concern:
The base of spine concerns itself with security
Below the naval concerns itself with pleasure
The solar plexus concerns itself with empowerment
The heart concerns itself with love
The throat concerns itself with communication
The third eye concerns itself with intuition
The crown concerns itself with Higher Self

The chakras connect to the body's nerve centers and glands
organs and emotions
Most importantly
they spin to the frequency of thoughts and beliefs
Communicating feelings and insights
Making known any blockages

If you have lower back pain
know you are not feeling secure
and the base of spine chakra is blocked

If you have hip pain or sexual imbalance
know you are not allowing pleasure
and your naval chakra is blocked

If you have a stomachache
know you have been giving up your power
and you solar plexus chakra is blocked

If you have heart and lung problems
know you are not embracing love in your life
and your heart chakra is blocked

If you have a sore throat
know you have not said what was needed
and the throat chakra is blocked

If you have eye problems or headaches
know you are not seeing what needs to be seen
and your third eye chakra is blocked

If you are feeling disconnected and alone
know you are not allowing the flow in from the higher realms
and your crown chakra is blocked

Each chakra is represented by a different color
Colors are light frequencies which project and attract
The chakras are frequencies of creation
Look to the beautiful colors in nature
and know the chakras are spinning

When the chakras are in balance
communication is clear and love is felt
insight is immediate and empowerment is yours to own

Alignment within the body
is alignment with the Earth and the Heavens
Thus
lighting the filament of existence

⚬

A map is a handy tool
It can give a detailed plan toward a location

The original idea of maps is to represent
the Inner Blueprint within the subtle realms of existence
Giving a detailed plan of the Becoming of all beings

Everything in the physical world symbolizes the
inner world or it would not exist

This is humanity's challenge
To attain this Sacred Knowledge
and develop the skills of a conscious mapmaker

Imagination is the bridge

The caterpillar has a blueprint of the butterfly
called imaginal cells
The human has a blueprint of its uniqueness
called *Soul's Dream*

The mapmaker understands the signposts of the Inner Blueprint
All leading to the origin of destination called desires
Using intuition for clarity

The mapmaker knows that all the routes lead to one destination
One destination only
Remembering
the mapmaker made the map

⤳⤳⤳

CHARLIE BOARDED THE TRAIN

Charlie had to catch a train. He was late and rushing down the street. "Nothing ever works for me!" Charlie said out loud to himself. "I am sick and tired of this life! I want some answers. Where is this God hiding? How does it work?"

At that moment, a large moving truck passed by. Big bold letters on the side of the truck stated:

"Get out of the way
We will do the work
Heavenly Movers, Inc."

Charlie briefly took notice of the truck and quickly dismissed it. "I want to know what to do with my life!" he cried waving his arms in the air and talking to himself. Passersby moved out of his way quickly, shaking their heads at his antics.

"What is the purpose of this life!" he cried aloud as he continued to walk down the street. Charlie stopped at a local bookshop and picked up a book on the sidewalk sale table. The title of the book was in bold red letters:

"Do What You Love
And Love Will Do For You
by The Foundation for a Better Life"

He mumbled and grunted and threw the book back down on the table. "Bullshit!" Charlie continued walking briskly down the street and passed an office with a sign hanging on the office door:

"Come To Me
Dr. Feelgood, MD"

He put his head down and continued walking. When he picked up his head another sign caught his attention:

**"Open
The Rabbit In The Hat Magic Store**
Magic is at your fingertips"

"Stupid store. What is the point of this life? All is such a ... "
He was interrupted by a little boy who fell off his bicycle. He looked at the boy indifferently and just stepped over the crying boy and continued ranting and raging under his breath. Absorbed in his complaining and not looking where he was going, he bumped into a traffic sign:

"Turn Around"

Something clicked for a moment, and he shook his head to get out of his daze. He turned around and squinted at the little boy ... there was a pause. He walked over to the boy and helped him up. Charlie brushed off the boy's clothes and picked up his bicycle. "Good as new," Charlie said. The boy looked into his eyes and smiled. Charlie watched the boy get on his bicycle and ride off. "What just happened?" he asked himself.

The sunlight seemed a bit brighter, and all the people passing Charlie were smiling at him. He even looked behind him, thinking they were all smiling at something else besides him.

With his head up, he walked slowly down the street and a butterfly landed on his shoulder. He turned his head and looked into the eyes of the butterfly. He noticed the bright, beautiful colors and the intricate design on its wings. "I don't think I ever really looked at a butterfly before," he said quietly. The butterfly flew off, and Charlie watched it until it disappeared into the blue sky.

He reached the railroad station and felt as though something had changed, something had shifted. He was very aware of his surroundings, and he felt he had received an answer, but to what, he wasn't sure. The only thing he was sure of was that he felt good. Charlie even smiled to himself. He searched his pocket for the train ticket and asked the conductor which track his train would be on.

The conductor replied, "You *are on the right track*." The conductor looked into Charlie's eyes and smiled as though he knew a secret that was just between himself and Charlie.

Charlie boarded the train, and his life was never the same.

Actions may appear to be the same
however
they are very different

A person looks at a flower
and sees a flower
Another looks at a flower
and sees the Universe

SACRED MOMENT ON HIGHER SELF

Higher Self is the consciousness and awareness that connects to *That* aspect which is a force greater than your personal self. It is a dose of the Absolute Self, a taste of the essence of your True Self connecting to the greater perspective of life.

We, as humans, cannot experience the whole experience of God or Absolute Self. We would explode with all the possibilities of *All That Is* and *All That Is Not*.

The Higher Self is a cup of the Eternal Ocean of Love experiencing *Satchitananda*, existence, knowledge, and bliss. Your Higher Self enables a glimpse into the *Omnipresent Infinite* while in the body.

MEDITATION

Gently close your eyes; inhale and exhale for three deep breath cycles. In your mind's eye, imagine walking down a beautiful, lush path lined with trees, plants, and flowers. You feel happy and excited. The path opens up to a clearing on a bay, ocean, or river beach. Look for a comfortable place to sit.

You hear a rustling in the woods coming toward you. You know who it is. With anticipated excitement, you await the arrival of your Higher Self.

Higher Self can be a luminous being, a feeling, an energy, a knowing, or just a sensing. Higher Self sits face-to-face with you, aligning with the third eye chakra, the area between your eyebrows. You are filled with love. You both gently and slowly move your heads toward each other, foreheads touching and hands holding.

Feel the connection and infusion from the Higher Self through your third eye chakra. Stay in this position. Feel the love through the hands and energy from infusion. The moment a thought enters your mind, the exchange is complete. It will be brief. Higher Self gently kisses your forehead.

Inhale and exhale slowly and gently open your eyes, and continue the day or evening with feelings of love from Higher Self.

IN CLOSING

I hope you had as much fun reading the *Heart Writings* as I did writing them. These writings contain subtle messages that speak to Soul for Heart to feel: the place where self and *Self* mingle.

Life is a fine-tuned balancing affair between Heaven and Earth, but it lives in the connection where they barely touch. Once known, the balancing affair becomes a love affair, and you fall in love with your life more each day.

Thank you for allowing me to express my love affair.

- *Om shanti.*

GLOSSARY

Absolute Self/Eternal Source: Supreme Consciousness; *I AM* Presence; God/Goddess.

All That Is: All of existence; Eternal Source; God; Quantum Field.

AUM/OM: The primordial/sacred sound and vibration that ignites creation; Sanskrit mantra in the Hindu/yogic traditions.

Conditioned world: The beliefs and attitudes shared by family, society, religion, and history that make up the belief system of mass consciousness and experienced as reality.

Chakras: Energy centers or vortices that are aligned with the spine. There are seven chakras within the body from the base of the spine to the crown of the head. The chakras are where the interaction between matter and consciousness meld. They are the bases for physical and emotional health, as well as connecting to higher states of consciousness and spirituality.

Dharma: Living within the cosmic flow and order (duties, virtues, spirituality) to uphold Existence.

Ego: The *I* that is identified with the body, mind, and senses; the personal self with likes and dislikes; the focal point of consciousness that navigates the body and personal mind through the physicality.

Eyeh Asher Eyeh: Famous verse in the Torah meaning *I AM who I AM. I AM is the* personal name for God; therefore, You are God.

Guru: Spiritual teacher who guides one to liberation.

I AM/Divine Identity: Individual Presence of the Eternal/Absolute Self; GodSelf.

Maya: Sanskrit word meaning the illusion or appearance of life. The illusion that all aspects of life are separate from you and are real. When the veil of *maya* is lifted, one is awakened.

Nadis: Subtle network within the body that distributes the life force; energy channels associated with the chakras and prana; there are 72,000 nadis.

Origin and Destiny: We merge from the non-physical at birth (Origin) and re-emerge into the non-physical at death (Destiny). Origin and Destiny come from the same Source.

Sage: An extremely wise person.

Sadhu (man); Sadhvis (woman): A seeker who chooses to renounce material possessions and society to focus on a spiritual life.

Satchitananda: Existence, knowledge (consciousness), and bliss is the experience attained by the illumined mind.

Self/yourSelf/Higher Self/True Self/GodSelf/You: Divine Consciousness that is within the individual; the higher vibration of consciousness that connects to *All That Is*, God, Creative Intelligence, etc.; the expansive perspective.

Sadhana- Spiritual practice to align with the inner self.

Soham: Sanskrit mantra meaning *I AM That;* I am the eternal.

Soul and Spirit: Soul is the *space* for passions, inspirations, and your true identity. Spirit is the *movement* that fills the *space* for creation; the *Becoming;* the divine marriage.

Tao: Ancient Chinese philosophy from the book *The Tao Te Ching* by Lao-Tzu. The Tao means the *way;* the *path* which encompasses the universe.

That: *Tat tvam asi –Thou art That;* Divine identity. You are the Eternal; God.

Yogi: One who practices yoga to reach liberation; self-actualization/enlightenment

Books by Stephanie Acello

Balancing the Stones
Mystical Writings to Wake Up Your Soul

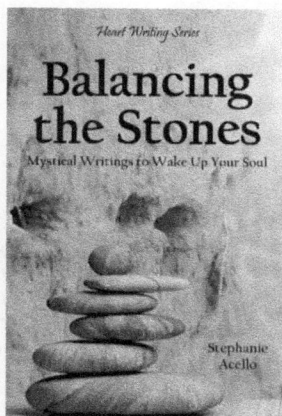

The second collection of mystical poetic insights and stories called *Heart Writings*-short, powerful, and inspirational writings to foster wonder and awareness about our lives and the world we live in. To deepen your awareness, at the end of each chapter you will find a *Sacred Moment Contemplation*. Allow these writings to energize your Soul and open your Heart. It is time to wake up!

Comments and Reviews

The overarching positive them is to "be the world you want to live in": which is a refreshing message compared to other works about meditation and contemplation. This book is a deep dive into what feels like the mystical world of the mind, and a great way to start the day. - Book Life Prize

...a must read for everyone wishing to form a deeper connection to the earth, spirit, and the authentic self. - SB

To order: stephanieacello.com or Amazon.com
For more information on upcoming books, talks, readings, and podcasts:
stephanieacello.com and www. facebook.com/onetonepublications/

ABOUT THE AUTHOR

Stephanie has been on the path of rediscovery her whole life, studying various practices and ideologies. Her practices included the principles of *Raja Yoga* while living within a community yoga ashram. She also participated in various intensive meditation and self-inquiry practices. She earned her Bachelor of Arts and Master of Science degrees in education and taught children and adults for many years.

She is a Certified Holistic Facilitator and Transformational Teacher, and taught small, intimate workshops entitled *The Secrets of Reality Unveiled*. Stephanie has also conducted *Heart Writing* readings in New York and Colorado.

The unique combination of her excellent teaching skills and insightful knowledge enables her to translate and communicate the *Inner Secrets* and *Data* of the *Mystical Realm*. Stephanie brings the *unknown* into the *known* with dynamic, inspirational, and profound simplicity.

Stephanie lives in beautiful Colorado with her family and friends. She operates a small fruit farm and enjoys her animal gurus.

www.ingramcontent.com/pod-product-compliance
Lightning Source LLC
Chambersburg PA
CBHW021038090426
42738CB00006B/144